THE BROTHERS' WAR

Despatches from the Heart

Lines of Battle: Letters from American Servicemen, 1941–1945

THE BROTHERS' WAR

— ★ —

CIVIL WAR LETTERS TO THEIR LOVED ONES FROM THE BLUE AND GRAY

EDITED BY

ANNETTE TAPERT

CIVIL WAR LIBRARY

VINTAGE BOOKS
A Division of Random House, Inc.
New York

FIRST VINTAGE BOOKS EDITION, November 1989

Copyright © 1988 by Annette Tapert

All rights reserved under International and Pan-American
Copyright Conventions. Published in the United States by
Vintage Books, a division of Random House, Inc., New York,
and simultaneously in Canada by Random House of Canada
Limited, Toronto. Originally published, in hardcover, by Times
Books, a division of Random House, Inc., New York, in 1988.

This copyright page is continued on pages 241–42.

LIBRARY OF CONGRESS CATALOGING-IN-PUBLICATION DATA
The Brothers' war : Civil War letters to their loved ones
from the Blue and Gray / edited by Annette Tapert. —
1st Vintage Books ed.
p.   cm.
Reprint. Originally published: New York : Times Books,
c1988.
Includes index.
ISBN 0-679-72211-4 : $8.95
1. United States—History—Civil War, 1861–1865—Personal
narratives.   2. Soldiers—United States—Correspondence.
I. Tapert, Annette.
[E601.B873   1989]
973.7'8—dc20   89-40078
                                                      CIP

Manufactured in the United States of America
10 9 8 7 6 5 4 3 2 1

EDITOR'S NOTE

My overriding criterion in selecting these letters was to find material that humanized the Civil War. Although some letters were chosen for their historical significance, the majority were selected for their lively prose style, emotional content, and anecdotal interest.

The letters have been arranged in chronological order to give the reader a sense of history. To allow the letters to speak simply for themselves, a very brief linking text provides a few background facts. In some cases, biographical information was not available, and those linking texts are, as a result, less detailed than I would have liked.

In many of these letters, the grammar is incorrect, the spelling is erratic, and the punctuation makes for awkward reading. For purposes of clarity, I have corrected spelling errors and, in some instances, streamlined the punctuation. A few of these letters have —due only to their length—been abridged.

The majority of the letters that appear in this anthology were selected from the outstanding collections at the Military History Institute at Carlisle Barracks in Carlisle, Pennsylvania. I want to thank Dr. Richard Sommers, the chief archivist-historian of the Institute, and his conscientious and courteous staff for all their assistance. I am also grateful to the staff of the Virginia Historical Society for their help.

It was not possible for me to deal singlehandedly with the voluminous amount of Civil War correspondence. I wish to thank Scott Hartwig for his invaluable help in the research and for sharing with me his encyclopedic knowledge of the subject.

On a more personal note, I am grateful to my friends and family for their never-ending support and enthusiasm.

INTRODUCTION

Louisa May Alcott, best known as the author of *Little Women*, made her literary debut with *Hospital Sketches*, a chronicle of her experiences as a Civil War nurse. In the mornings, she tended to the wounded and sprinkled lavender over them to cover the smells of sickness and poor sanitation. Once she had completed those tasks, she took pen to paper and began her final duty of the day, "to minister to their minds by writing letters to the anxious souls at home."

"The letters dictated to me," she recalled in her book, "would have made an excellent chapter for some future history of the war; they were 'full of affection, pluck, and bad spelling,' nearly all giving lively accounts of battle, and ending with a somewhat sudden plunge from patriotism to provender, desiring 'Marm,'

'Mary Ann,' or 'Aunt Peters' to send along some pies, pickles, sweet stuff, and apples, 'to yourn in haste,' Joe, Sam, or Ned, as the case may be."

"From patriotism to provender"—that seemed, from the vantage point of 1863, to describe the range of concerns of the average soldier. More than a century later, we can see that the men who fought the Civil War were concerned with much more than the sanctity of their cause and their need for some of the comforts of home. Indeed, from their letters we can chart a deeper progression from simple belief to more complex feelings—and to doubt and despair.

"The faith is true and adorable," wrote Oliver Wendell Holmes, Jr., of his Civil War experiences, "which leads a soldier to throw away his life in obedience to a blindly accepted duty, in a cause which he little understands, in a plan of campaign of which he has no notion, under tactics of which he does not see the use." At the end of the twentieth century, such faith is bewildering—but the first revelation of the letters in this book is how deeply the soldiers on both sides embraced their causes. Despite the fact that they were mostly young farmers and small-town boys who were separated from their families for the first time, these soldiers don't speak often—in the first years of the war, anyway—of homesickness. For them, leaving home was an adventure. Danger was an intoxicant. And the opportunities to prove themselves heroes were boundless. "The Lord," Herman Melville proclaimed in a Civil War poem, "is a man of war!"

At the beginning of the war, nothing could shake this certainty. Letter after letter testifies to the soldiers' strength of character. Rank, for them, was of less importance than a man's inner qualities. A Confederate soldier writes, after the First Battle of Bull Run, of his introduction to battle: "The balls make a very loud singing noise when they pass near you, and it at first caused me to duck my head, but I soon became used to it. I never expected to be alarmed or excited in battle, but really it is a very different affair from what I thought it. I never was cooler in my life, and have ever since been very much pleased therefore, as I shall have no trouble hereafter." Even a Union soldier whose comrades had been routed in that same battle could find reason for pride. "A great many claim the credit of protecting the retreat and being the last to leave the field," he writes. "But it is all in the imagination, for *we were the last to leave Centreville.*"

What is most impressive about these Civil War letters is how alike they sound, how little difference there is between the sentiments of Union and Confederate men. As we know, when they weren't fighting, the soldiers from opposing sides could be astonishingly friendly, trading tobacco for newspapers and swimming together. But they were most alike in their moral certainty—each side believed in the absolute rightness of its cause. As Melville wrote:

> *Like snows the camps on Southern hills*
> *Lay all the winter long,*
> *Our levies there in patience stood—*
> *They stood in patience strong.*
> *On fronting slopes gleamed other camps*
> *Where faith as firmly clung:*
> *Ah, froward kin! so brave amiss—*
> *The zealots of the Wrong.*

What Melville and the authors of these early letters did not understand is that the outcome of the war would depend less on moral superiority than on supplies, railroads, and munitions.

In this, the Civil War was the first modern war. It had, therefore, two fronts—the battlefield and the factory. On the battlefield, the Confederacy may be said to have prevailed: Confederate troops killed 365,000 Union soldiers while losing 258,000 of their own. And Confederate strategy was sufficiently sophisticated that, in the 1930's, German officers journeyed to America to tour the Southern battlefields in order to refine their own tank tactics. But on the industrial front, the Confederacy had no chance for victory. It had eight thousand miles of railroad to the Union's twenty-two thousand miles. And the South had only 10 percent of the nation's industrial jobs.

By late 1862, the letter-writers begin to understand that the war won't be over quickly and that, whoever wins, the toll on the victor will be nearly as heavy as it will be for the vanquished. For the first time, we hear Confederate soldiers writing: "I have had enough of the glory of war. I am sick of seeing dead men and men's limbs torn from their bodies. . . . When the war ends, if I am alive, no one will return to peaceful avocations more willingly than I." At Antietam, we find a soldier confessing to his family what he cannot admit to his comrades: "When . . . just as they were ready to come down on us, and before we had a chance to complete our change of front, I saw them haul up a battery in the same place and plant it, I am frank to confess that although I had no idea of running away, I trembled."

At the beginning of the war, moral standards were so high that if, for example, a Confederate soldier was captured and there were no Union troops to escort him to a prisoner-of-war camp, he was often trusted to make his way there on his own. But by late 1862, we begin to see letter-writers noting the erosion of these standards. The Confederates, one writer claims, hoist a Union flag to deceive their enemies. Dead Rebels are found dressed in Union uniforms. In addition to rifling the pockets of the dead and stealing their shoes, the Confederates loot the dead of their family pictures.

As this behavior becomes more common, morale is affected. Letters home no longer tell only of battle glory and camp life. Now we find soldiers describing the drumming out of deserters: "The prisoner was called out, his head shaven, the iron heated, pants turned down and brand applied, the army buttons cut off his clothes—a squad of soldiers with fixed bayonets played behind him when the band struck up the 'rogues' march.' " But the writer's disgust is now tempered by realism. His letter ends with the comment, "I have concluded not to desert this week at least."

Such despair is perhaps a minority opinion. As the price of glorious battle became clear, most soldiers wrapped themselves more deeply in their faith—both as Christians and as partisans. We find, in 1863, a New York soldier writing: "There were many brave men who saw the last of earth on that battlefield of Chancellorsville, and many tears will flow, for many a year. But what are these tears to the bitter ones a mother sheds over an erring son, out of whom everything good has died, and only his body lives?" And, after the Battle of Gettysburg, we cannot fail to be impressed by a soldier's letter to his mother in which he describes the death of his only brother: "He died as he would have died—with his face toward the enemies of freedom, on the battlefield." This letter becomes even more poignant when we discover that soon after this letter was mailed, its author was taken prisoner. Three months later, he was dead.

The variety of opinions we discover in the letters of Civil War soldiers is due, in large part, to the freedom of the camps. Except in some prison camps, there was no censorship of soldiers' letters, and officers knew how valuable letters could be in preventing homesickness and malingering. In the early days of the war, family visits were permitted, and a surprising number of soldiers surrounded themselves with valets brought from home and relatives who made vacations out of their visits to camp. The frequency of civilian contact—impossible in modern armies—is one reason that soldiers frequently note in their letters how little training they actually receive. If men had to learn how to fight on the battlefield, that is yet another reason why they relied so strongly on their faith and character to see them through.

There is another, blessedly human side to these war letters—the raucous, gossipy recollections of the social experiences of war. Soldiers visit the home of a fine family and infest its sofas with lice. Practical jokes are recounted, personal grievances are vented. And just when we are in danger of concluding that war lowers the morality of all its participants, a Confederate officer writes home about a prisoner in his care, a man so hungry that he would trade a silver pocket flask for a piece of bread. "I told him if he would promise not to try to escape, I would take him out to breakfast," he writes. "He readily promised, and away we went over hill and dale together without even a pistol, chattering gaily as we promenaded together. We reached the house and got a splendid breakfast. The old lady and her daughters saw my old gray uniform and the yankee's dark blue cloth and they stirred about like the house was on fire."

Paradoxically, it is letters like these that bring home the full tragedy of the brothers' war. To us, that is. To the soldiers who fought the Civil War, it was precisely these moments—and the pumped-up glory of the bugles and the guns—that made this bloodiest of all American wars so lovingly remembered. It was too painful for the veterans of this war to look back upon the carnage and the waste. They wrapped their letters in ribbons and put them in the trunk in the attic, and then reinvented the war as the religious crusade they wished it had been.

Decades later, when their children unwrapped their letters, they must have been surprised—even shocked—to discover how grim and wasteful this great adventure had really been. But despite a stream of books that have made the War Between the States the most documented conflict in our history, these later generations also succumbed to myth, in the form of the romantic revisionism of such books as *Gone With the Wind*. In our own time, the Civil War is widely regarded as a kind of pageant, and every year enthusiasts dress up in uniforms to reenact, with Rebel yells and Union songs, the great charges of Shiloh and Gettysburg.

To these memories and distortions, volumes of Civil War letters are a corrective. They present the war in the much-loved vernacular of the common soldier. They are immediate, and they are powerfully felt. Like all combat letters, they offer a parallel history of war—a blood-soaked chronicle of experience from ground level. Reading them, we can begin to understand not only the passion and stoicism of these soldiers, but their need to obscure and even reinvent their memories.

ANNETTE TAPERT

New York, New York
March 1988

THE BROTHERS' WAR

Typical interior of a soldier's quarters

— ★ —

The following letter was written by John Esten Cooke to his close friend and relative "J.E.B." Stuart, who at the time was serving as a lieutenant in the United States Army in Kansas. Cooke, who enlisted as an artillerist in the Confederate Army shortly after Virginia withdrew from the Union, later became Major General Stuart's ordnance officer. While serving, Lieutenant Cooke also wrote wartime columns for the Southern Illustrated News *and published* Life of Stonewall Jackson *in 1863. After the war, Cooke wrote five war-related books.*

April 4th, 1861

DEAR LIEUTENANT:

I received your short letter some time ago and ought to have answered it sooner. Better late than never however, and now I have something to say.

I will first tell you that your mother is quite well and in excellent spirits. She and myself are great friends, and I called on her this afternoon. . . .

But to the subject of my letter. I have commenced in rather a jesting way, but I assure you, my dear friend, that I have very serious intent in this letter. I mean to show you some important things from this point of view, and try and make you of my way of thinking—namely that the moment has come for you and Uncle to *act promptly* and curtail events that are nearly on us.

I don't intend to go into any talk about the Lincoln government and that at Montgomery. I have no doubt that you despise the one and admire the other as much as I do. But I say—the time is imminently here at hand when you and Uncle will be aides and abettors of the sworn foes—and active foes—of your country (I mean the South, for that is your country) and your own kindred. Virginia is as certain for secession as anything in the future can be. She will join the Confederate states—and my hope of reconstruction is visionary. Do you intend to wait? I will tell you what you will gain by that. The prizes in the Southern Army will all be drawn and you will have the place of the laggard. The commissions are being given every day. I will mention an instance. My friend Edwin Harris—son of Louis E. Harris, of Amelia, and Lieutenant, 9th Infantry—without *letters of recommendation,* and on simple application, received the 10th captaincy in '60. I saw the making of the whole affair from the start and there was no extraneous influence brought to bear upon his promotion. He was advanced on a fixed policy—and from an inspection of the list of Captains. I am certain that the *policy of that government* is to hold out the strongest inducements to the army officers from border (not yet seceded) states —with the plain political object of encouraging Southern feeling therein by the disposition now shown to entrust border statesman with places of trust and involvement. . . .

Unquestionably you and Uncle would resign "on account of the secession of the Confederate States" and you would "of course" receive equal commissions in the Southern Army—but that is not all. Captain Harvie—and this is in confidence for you and Uncle alone—says that the policy there (at Montgomery, from which he has just returned) is to advance officers resigning, one grade. He expresses the belief that Uncle would be made one of the Brigadiers, if prompt application were made—as I am certain as I am of my existence that you could be either Major or Captain—probably the former, certainly the latter. The unfortunate part of the affair is that you and Uncle are at the end of the world. They are in the West and, I suppose, if a bloody battle were fought in the Atlantic States, would not hear of it for weeks.

I express my convictions that under all the circumstances the dictate of good policy of every feeling of the Southerner and the soldier is—resign at once and go to this noble government of the South . . .

I do not think that ever in my life I expressed myself more confusedly, awkwardly and badly. But I believe I have, one way or another, put down some of the main points. Remain with the Lincoln humbug and political farce government, you and Uncle cannot. He's a foreign despotism to you and to me. I'll fight against it if the time for fighting comes. I, with hundreds more, bound ourselves the other day by reaching agreement to resist by force of arms that government and the government of Virginia too, and stop the new Federal guns from balloon arsenals up the river on their way to Fort Monroe; the fight may commence here at any moment. It will come if we do not secede as sure as fate, and then you and Uncle are sworn to put us to the bayonet at the orders of Scott and Lincoln. . . .

I have written freely and frankly, my dear friend. I regard you as a friend and cousin. I believe that I counsel the path of interest and honor. Get Uncle's authority to act for him and come east at once if Colonel Sumner will let you. I beg you to answer this at once. Speak plainly as I do—I have used no ceremony. This is not the time for it. We are in revolution and events rush on too wildly for ceremony. I beseech you to communicate at once with Uncle to where I've written, and come east and judge for yourself.

Love to all, yours faithfully,
John E. Cooke

— ★ —

Less than three weeks after the firing on Fort Sumter, war was declared. William Darst had already heeded the call for volunteers to defend Virginia, and enlisted in the 21st Virginia Volunteer Infantry.

Camp of Instruction
May 3, '61
Hermitage Fair Grounds Camp

My Dear Ma:

I received your kind and affectionate letter day before yesterday. I was very anxious to hear from home and to know how you were all getting along. I expect it is right lonely since Jack and I left. I never get lonesome here surrounded by about four thousand men, of all kinds. We get along very well here, never have any disturbances at all, except at night sometimes the guard take people to the watch house. There is a guard of one hundred men detailed from the different companies every night, which are divided into five different watches and each watch stands two hours before it is relieved by the next succeeding one. The cadets have the guard under their care, the reason is they are so much better acquainted with military duty than anyone else in camp.

Everything moves as regularly here as if moved by machinery. The drum beats at five to get up. At ten minutes after, the roll is called, at six the drill begins, ends at seven, and breakfast at eight and drill at nine, ends at ten, commences again at eleven and ends at twelve, dinner at one and then we have a recess until three, when drill commences again and ends at four, dress parade at sundown. The people of Richmond turn out by the thousands to see this, they assemble onto seats erected on the race course. It is a beautiful sight to see four thousand soldiers in full uniform forming the hollow square with a thousand on each side. . . .

You must all make yourselves easy about us. I expect your anxiety is harder to bear than our hardships. . . .

Write soon, give my love to Mrs. Sumner, tell me everything that is going on in the neighborhood.

Yours affectionately,
Wm. B. Darst

— ★ —

Thomas Lightfoot was mustered into Company A, 6th Alabama Volunteer Infantry, as second lieutenant on May 11, 1861. This is his first letter home.

Camp Davis near Corinth, Miss.
May 29th, 1861

Dear Cousin:

We arrived here several days ago, but I have been so wearied that I was not able to write to you. I will now give you my views of a soldier's life.

A soldier is worse than any negro on Chattahoochee River. He has no privileges whatever. He is under worse task-masters than any negro. He is not treated with any respect whatever. His officers may insult him and he has no right to open his mouth and dare not do it. My officers have always treated me with the utmost courtesy, and I expect will always treat me so, for I am going to obey orders. This is a hard life, but I like it very much. We make our pallets on the ground and we rise at the tap of the drum or we are placed on double duty. I have been so fortunate as to be always at my post.

We left Montgomery on Saturday last in very good 1st class passenger cars, and were getting along finely until we got to Chattanooga, where they placed us in box cars. Ladies crowded to every little depot to cheer us on [our] way. I can truly say I never saw as many and as pretty ladies in my life as there is on the road from Montgomery to Corinth. The cars were literally covered with bouquets from the beautiful ladies. I think when I want a wife I will come somewhere on this road to find her.

It is generally supposed down in our country that the people of North Alabama are not right on the present issue, but I can assure you that they are the most warlike people I have ever seen. Women cheer us, and the men go along with us. Every little village has at least twenty-five flags floating aloft.

You must write to me soon and give me all the news. Give my love to Uncle, Dr. and Lady, and all the rest of the family and accept the wishes of your most obedient servant and affectionate cousin,

T. R. LIGHTFOOT

— ★ —

Eugene Blackford* served as a major with the 5th Alabama Volunteer Infantry. His letter was written the day after the first great battle of the war—the First Battle of Bull Run.

Bivouac Camp of the Advanced Guard,
on the railroad near Union Mills
Above Manassas
22nd July, 1861

MY DEAR FATHER:
We are very much fatigued and jaded by our late movements. I must relieve your anxiety by letting you know that I am alive and well. I was in the great battle of yesterday, tho our regt. arrived too late to take any considerable part in the action. But I will go back and let you know what I have been doing since this day a week.

*Another letter by Eugene Blackford appears on page 197.

Last Monday the enemy advanced their lines considerably and caused our pickets to fall back some two miles. We were up all Tuesday night expecting to march down to the battery to defend it. At 8 o'clock Wednesday, the advance guard of the enemy appeared, and we went out to give battle. We all took our positions behind our entrenchments, and remained there some time while parties of our men were skirmishing in front.

At last they were driven in, and the firing commenced upon our line. The enemy, having minie muskets, could fire upon us long before we could think of returning the compliment, and so we had to take it coolly. No wound was sustained by our men (in my company) except one pretty badly wounded. The balls make a very loud singing noise when they pass near you, and at first caused me to duck my head, but I soon became used to it. I never expected to be alarmed or excited in battle, but really it is a very different affair from what I thought it. I never was cooler in my life, and have ever since been very much pleased therefore, as I shall have no trouble hereafter.

Just as we were about to make our fire general, news was brought that the [Illinois] had retreated from Fairfax Court House and thus had exposed our flank. Of course there was nothing to be done but to retreat. This we barely had time to do, the enemy was almost in sight of the crossroads when we passed at double quick. Had we been twenty minutes later, we would have been cut off utterly. As I said before, we marched quick time for twenty miles to this place, my company being deployed as skirmishers on the side next to the enemy. The part was one of honor and implied trust, but it was at a great cost, as the country was awfully rough, and we suffered very much.

Ever since, we have been here at work making batteries to defend the passage of Bull Run. I have a ford to defend and have thrown up a very nice battery for about fifty yards. We worked with arms by our sides, expecting an attack at any moment from the Yankees, who were about two miles off.

Yesterday morning, about daylight, word was brought that the enemy was advancing on all sides, and that we must be ready to advance to the support of any point that might be seriously threatened. We had an alarm about 8 o'clock and set out immediately, but were ordered back before we had proceeded far, because the order was countermanded. We stood some eight hours in the sun on the road awaiting further orders. Since seven in the morning, heavy cannonading has been heard on all sides, mingled with a perfect roar of musketry. At eleven o'clock we set off at double quick to reinforce our men at Mitchell's Ford and so, after crossing a dozen creeks, in the same creek a dozen times, we came upon the enemy. While retreating, they had been informed of our coming and had set off double quick, so we had our march of three miles for nothing.

We then came right about and set off to reinforce our men in the great battle (not yet named) about ten miles from us. This distance we marched at double time and came on the field about five o'clock, too late as I said to do much service, but early enough to smell a little gunpowder and receive a little of the enemy's fire. We went over the battlefield several miles in extent. T'was truly awful, an immense cloud of smoke and dust hung over the whole country, and the flashing of the artillery was incessant tho none of the balls struck my company. One bomb burst a little above me, and killed and wounded several. This was our only loss. Had we been an hour earlier, many would not have lived to tell of it.

I shan't attempt to describe the appearance of the field, literally covered with bodies, and for five miles before reaching it I saw men limping off, more or less wounded. We met wagon loads of bodies coming off to Manassas, where they are now piled in heaps. While we were looking over the field, an order came for us to go back to our batteries ten miles off, and defend them from the enemy who were advancing upon them, so we had to go back, tired as we were, to our holes, where we arrived half dead at twelve o'clock last night, having marched twenty-six miles heavily loaded. We have no protection against the rain, which has been falling all day. I have no blanket, not having seen my baggage since leaving Fairfax; I never was so dirty before in my life and besides I have scurvy in my mouth, not having anything but hard bread and intensely salty meat to eat, and not enough of that.

I do not however complain, nor do my men, tho I never thought that such hardships were to be endured. We have our meat in the blaze, and eat it on our bread. A continual firing is now going on around us.

> Your affectionate son,
> EUGENE BLACKFORD

— ★ —

At the First Battle of Bull Run, Philip Powers* was serving as a sergeant major with the 1st Virginia Cavalry. He later became a captain in the Quartermaster Department, Cavalry Corps, Confederate Army of Northern Virginia.

> Camp at Fairfax Courthouse
> July 23, 1861

MY DEAREST WIFE:

Several Clark men, among them Knelles, were in our camp for a short time this evening but I was so busy I had not time even to drop you a line, and fearing lest the same thing may occur again, I write tonight, though excessively fatigued.

Yesterday we had a drenching rain all day and most of last night, and being without our tents we could not escape the rain and mud. We broke our camp however about midnight and marched to this place accompanied by two regiments of infantry and one battery of artillery. I was glad to leave, for as I wrote you we were near by a hospital of the enemy where [there were] over three hundred of their wounded, dead and dying. Many of them necessarily left out in all the inclemency of weathers to die. To pass by it was enough to soften and sicken the hardest heart. I will not dwell upon the awful scene.

*Another letter by Philip Powers appears on page 199.

The battle was nothing to this after piece. The excitement of the contest, the cheering of the soldiers, the triumph of victory and the whole field of many of its terrors—*nothing* could lessen the horrors of the field by moonlight. Enough—I cannot, I will not describe it. May God, in his infinite mercy, avert a second such calamity. Our march after we got beyond the scenes of the fight was rather cheering than otherwise. For twelve miles the road was literally strewn with every description of baggage, wagons, ambulances, barrels of sugar, crackers, ground coffee and thousands of axes, spades, shovels, picks, arms by the thousands, clothing of every description, cooking utensils—in fact, everything—and all left behind to expedite their flight, which was never stopped until they reached Washington.

Our troops have been busily engaged in appropriating everything they might possibly need, from a pin cushion to the finest army tent. In this place we found in several houses clothing enough to fill every room in our house. Their army was splendidly equipped with every possible convenience and comfort. But I cannot account for their utter confusion and panic. Their own papers give our regiment the credit of turning the tide of victory on our side. The papers if you can see them will give you all particulars . . .

An example of a troop's winterized quarters in Virginia

I do not know what our next move will be but suppose it will be upon Alexandria. All I desire is to drive them from our soil and secure peace—I would not shed another drop . . .

I cannot write now. Farewell! I pray that my wife and little children may be protected and comforted at all times.

> Ever Yours,
> P. H. POWERS

— ★ —

At the time of writing, Robert McAllister was serving as a lieutenant colonel with the 1st New Jersey Volunteer Infantry. By October of 1864, he had attained the rank of brevet brigadier general. The following letter was written after the First Battle of Bull Run.

> 1st N.J. Volunteers
> Fort Albany
> July 25, 1861

FRIEND WIESTLING:

In writing to you yesterday I had to stop short, as the cry was: "The enemy are coming." But it turned out to be only a troop of horse. Fire was exchanged and they disappeared.

The right wing of our Regiment have since been engaged in throwing up breastworks at the Arlington Mills, some three miles out from the river at a road and railroad crossing, where we are planting a battery to sweep the road. We hope the North will pour down her troops so that before long we may take up our line of march to Centreville and Manassas Junction and regain what we have lost.

No retreat should have been ordered at Bull Run, for the day was ours. The enemy were whipped. The men fought brave enough, but we have too many cowardly officers. Yet we have very many brave ones who did credit to our arms.

Sabbath morning, July 21st, the 1st and 2nd New Jersey Volunteers were encamped at Vienna. Col. McLean commanded the 2nd

LIEUTENANT ROBERT McALLISTER

New Jersey. Being Lieutenant Colonel of the 1st Regiment, I commanded that unit, as our Col. Montgomery outranked McLean and thus had command of the whole.

The roaring of artillery announced the opening of the battle of Bull Run. Three of our companies were absent on reconnaissance and had not returned when orders came from Headquarters for us to move up to Centreville. We were soon on our way and moving rapidly toward the scene of conflict. We passed Germantown, the artillery sounding louder and louder. Some miles on this side of Centreville, we met a gentleman who said all was right, the enemy were driven in toward Manassas Gap. On we went, feeling elated. After a while, the artillery ceased firing. We then knew that the battle was decided; but which way was the question.

Soon this sad story was told by the confused mass of the retreating army. We determined to do what we could to stop the panic. We threw our columns across the road, appealed to their patriotism, to their honor, to the Flag, and urged them to return and help us fight the battle. But the panic was so great that our appeals were for the time unheeded. We then charged bayonets and stopped the stampede, letting only the wounded pass on.

We turned into our ranks about five hundred of the stampeders, then marched through their retreating columns. We drew our swords and pistols on men and officers who would not willingly turn back. The whole scene beggars all description; and yet, strange to say, our officers and men were all cool. We marched through those retreating columns with a firmness which astonished all who saw the Regiment—and which has since been the topic of universal praise. Had I time, I could give you some singular instances, several of which were amusing even amid the sad spectacle around us. . . .

Cheer after cheer went up for us as we advanced, and solemn promises were made on the part of the stampeders that they would fall in our rear if we advanced through them and formed a line of battle. Others cried: "Go up yonder hill and you'll get it! You will be cut to pieces!" Still others encouraged us with hopes that we would save their retreat and bear the brunt of the battle.

The stampede was now stopped and we were on the summit of a hill. Col. Montgomery had a conference with Genl. McDowell and urged the propriety of making a stand on the heights of Centreville—throwing up breastworks, holding the position, and not retreating to Washington. The General consented and ordered him to take his command to the other side of Centreville and form his lines for defense. We passed Centreville and took up a position on the hill with our right resting on the road along which the enemy would have to come. But when we had accomplished this and were ready for battle, we found that our 2nd New Jersey Regiment had retreated. Two regiments under the command of Col. Blenker were the only troops left besides. . . .

Having placed pickets out to give the alarm, the men lay down on their arms. Col. Montgomery and myself began to look around to see what was going on. We had a consultation with the colonel of a New York regiment—one of those under the command of Blenker—and we concluded to fight and stand by each other. We returned to our Regiment. An hour passed away in silence. We then thought we heard something. On examination we found that our neighboring troops were moving off and that we alone would be in possession of the field. Now came the question: what are we to do?

We concluded to take another position around the lower hospital and across the road along which the Rebels would have to come. We reformed in the new position but left the road clear. Yet we so arranged our forces as to sweep the road with a raking fire in case the cavalry came. I . . . waited in silence. Col. Montgomery and Maj. Hatfield left to call on Genl. McDowell, who was two miles off, to learn why Blenker's two regiments had left us alone, and to find out what was to be done.

After sitting some time on my horse in silence—the men having nearly all fallen asleep—I passed over to the left wing on the other side of the road in order to throw out additional pickets. One of our Captains asked me if I knew the danger we were in.

"Certainly," I replied.

"Why don't we retreat?" he then asked.

I told him my orders were to hold this position and that I was going to do it.

"We may as well surrender all at once," he said, "as we will be cut to pieces."

I told him we would never surrender and that we would give them a tremendous fight.

I then returned to my position and remained there until Maj. Hatfield returned and informed me that we had to retreat. Our orders were given in a low tone, almost a whisper. . . .

As we marched from Centreville, we had our rear column in a condition to defend. Cavalry was what we most feared. After marching several miles, we reached the rear of the retreating column and thus protected them until we arrived at Fairfax, when we took a more advanced position for some miles. Afterward we formed protection for a battery and reached this place about two P.M. Monday, worn out and terrible hungry. We had not eaten anything for thirty hours save a dry piece of bread when we were in line of battle at Centreville. Almost all that time we were on duty. Our horses had nothing to eat and no time to eat. Worn out by fatigue, many of our men sank down on the roadside and could not even be forced along. They lay all night in a pelting storm. The ambulances had all left. Remember that all wagons save twenty or thirty had left us; and of those, the drivers had cut loose their horses and ridden off at great speed. . . .

I do contend that we—i.e., all the army—ought to have formed at Centreville according to Montgomery's idea. Had that plan been pursued, we would be in possession of it yet.

A great many claim the credit of protecting the retreat and being the last to leave the field. But it is all in the imagination, for *we were the very last to leave Centreville.* In confidence I tell you that when our Colonel called on Genl. McDowell, he could not be found. He had retreated without giving us orders to retreat, and we would have been left to be cut to pieces had we not accidentally discovered that Col. Blenker was retreating. You see it stated that Blenker's command saved the retreat, and yet we were in Centreville two hours after Col. Blenker left.

I have now given a fair, unvarnished statement of the whole matter, but have been so much interrupted that I fear it will be uninteresting. . . .

— ★ —

At the age of forty-five, Samuel Beardsley joined the 24th New York Volunteer Infantry, attaining the rank of lieutenant colonel.

Near Washington
Sept. 12, 1861

MY DEAR FREDDY:

I wrote your mother quite a long letter on Friday last and a short one on Saturday enclosing a draft for $100, which I trust came safely to hand. On Sunday, I left camp with five companies (about three hundred men) for Bailey's Cross Roads, about which place you will see a good deal said in the papers, as it is in close proximity to the rebels, and a skirmish takes place in that vicinity about every day.

My scouts made an important discovery on Sunday evening, to wit, an encampment of the enemy close by where one of my companies was picketed, and a good deal nearer than they had dared to come heretofore. There appeared to be four or five companies. The next morning while taking observations from the roof of a deserted house on an elevated position, I discovered the enemy at work on a new fortification which no one had seen before, and by the aid of a glass I could almost see the features of the different men, white and black.

About the same time, a smart skirmish commenced immediately back of the house where I was, between one company of the Rochester Regiment and two companies of rebels. I sent word to the Rochester boys that if they needed assistance I would be with them with my company in five minutes, but they sent word back that they would rather whip them alone. The firing lasted about an hour and the last I heard the Union troops were driving the rebels before them towards Falls Church, where they are pretty strong.

All these skirmishes are intended by the enemy to try to draw us outside of our entrenchments, and have a big battle, but this they cannot do until Gen. McClellan gives the word. Washington is now considered impregnable, there being a continuous line of fortifications on this side of the river, for fifteen miles. These forts are some of them very large (one in particular, Fort Runyon, is calculated to require ten thousand men to man it properly), and have been built almost entirely by the troops. There is no spot for fifteen miles up and down the river that is not commanded by our cannon, and I would like to see Beauregard attempt to take Washington with all the force he can bring into the field. We should make mince meat of him in short order.

Shortly after I discovered the new fortifications of the enemy on Monday morning, I met Brig. Gen. Wadsworth, who deemed the discovery so important, as well as the discovery of their new camp the evening before, that he sent me immediately to report the facts to Gen. McDowell and Gen. Keyes, the commander of our Brigade. They both complimented me very highly upon my "prudence and watchfulness" and seemed highly pleased at being put in possession of the information so promptly. All day Sunday we could see the enemy at their finished fortifications on Munson's Hill and in the afternoon saw them hold services outside of the Fort, at which several ladies were present.

While we were out, Levi's company (part of them) had a skirmish with the enemy. Your Uncle Levi had a rifle and took deliberate aim at one of the rebels at a distance so short that he could have sent him to eternity in a second, but he says he could not fire on a man in that murderous fashion, and he dropped his gun, letting the rascal go. I think he did right, although they shoot our troops every opportunity they get. But because they murder men is no reason why we should do the same. In battle it would be different and I would be killing as many of them as possible.

I have never shot but once at any of them, and I felt ashamed of myself a moment afterwards. He was a sentry posted on the roof of a house, more than half a mile off, and I had no expectation of hitting him and was delighted when I saw how nimbly he jumped behind the chimney after I fired, showing that he was not hurt, although my ball must have struck the roof close to him. Our Enfield rifles are a terrible weapon, being able to kill a man at the distance of a mile. Only one other regiment besides ours has them and the rebels have learned to give our 24th boys a wide birth.

Captain Miller's company also had a skirmish when we were out. None of our men were injured. How it was with the enemy we could not tell. I write all this, expecting all hands will have the benefit of it and presuming you will all feel interested in knowing how I got through my outpost duty, about which I wrote to your mother on Friday.

On Monday, after I got back, I was seized by my old enemy, Mr. Diarrhea, and on Tuesday was very sick. Dr. Murdock gave me about half a tea cup full of castor oil, which has done me some good, and I have today commenced taking tincture of iron, three times a day, and quinine twice a day. It is to give me strength, I believe. Dr. M. says I ought to go home for about three weeks and recruit up, but I don't suppose this would be possible. He attributes my sickness in a great measure to sleeping in a damp tent, but I am today going to have a floor laid, which will obviate this difficulty. I attribute this last attack to eating a large quantity of pickled oysters while we were at Bailey's Cross Roads. Uncle Levi gave me a can of them and, being hungry, I ate freely of them, together with a goodly quantity of cheese, ginger cakes and sweet biscuit. It was imprudent, but it is so seldom that I have anything so tempting that, being quite hungry, I pitched in.

Today I feel nearly well; indeed, I was well enough yesterday to attend a short battalion drill in the forenoon and a review of our Brigade in the afternoon at which Gen. Butler and Secy. Seward were present. Our Brigade is composed of four tip-top regiments, and Gen. Keyes feels very proud of his command. It is without exception the finest looking brigade this side of the Potomac and every one speaks of "Keyes' Brigade" in the highest terms. I hope if the time ever comes when they are to be baptized in fire, that they won't forfeit the good reputation they now enjoy. . . .

Evening: I had to stop writing to attend to battalion drill, but as this cannot be mailed before tomorrow, it makes no difference. I have also put down a floor in my tent of nice clean boards, which Dr. Murdock gave me, he having made a requisition for some lumber for hospital purposes, and had enough left to make himself a floor for his tent and enough for me besides. With my new tent and my new floor, I am quite comfortable and it really begins to look like housekeeping.

Last night we had a pouring rain and I got up to tighten the curtains of my tent when I stepped, splash, into a puddle of water which had run in. I have tried for more than a week to get lumber

An officer of the 3rd Pennsylvania Cavalry, camped near Westover, Virginia, takes a break in August 1862.

for a floor, but everything that would answer, board fences and all, are snapped up the minute a regiment locates itself, and our present camp has been occupied by three or four regiments before us. To show how difficult it is to obtain lumber, one of our officers had to pay $5.00 the other day for enough to floor a small tent about a third as large as mine.

You ought to see some of my furniture; for instance, my outdoor washstand consists of a stake driven in the ground with a barrel head nailed on the top. I also have a one-legged stool made of a small barrel head nailed onto a short stake. My writing desk is made of a large dry goods box in which I have made a shelf, where I keep my writing materials, candle sticks and candles, books, tumbler, matches, brushes, soap, a paper of nails and tacks, bottles of medicines, etc.—one of the most capacious as well as convenient shelves you ever saw.

Our eating arrangements are very poor but the best we can get. Two of the soldiers have established a sort of boarding tent where we get most vile coffee, butter strong enough to walk alone, and meat of some sort generally for breakfast and dinner. The bread is always excellent but that is about all that will bear commendation. It comes awful tough to live this way, but it is so much ahead of our living for the three weeks we lay at Arlington Mills that we feel quite contented.

I long for the box you sent by Mr. Gallagher, hoping to find some relishes, like anchovy paste or brandy cheese or something of that sort, that I can occasionally lunch upon like a Christian. . . .

I hope to get a long letter tomorrow, advising that the money I sent has arrived safely. Give my love to Grandma and tell her I congratulate her on her seventy-first birthday and trust she will see many more. Tell Mary, with my love, that I will write her before long.

From your affectionate
FATHER

— ★ —

John Holloway served as a private with Company G, 1st Georgia Volunteer Infantry. His letter home was written after seeing action at the Battle of Cheat Mountain, West Virginia, on September 11–13, 1861.

———

Camp Bartow
September 19, 1861

DEAR MISS BETTIE:

This morning I seat myself to acknowledge the reception of your kind letter that came to hand yesterday. I am still in fine health and spirits, a blessing that but few of my comrades can boast. You will perceive that our army had moved from the place that we were at when I wrote to you last. I am now thirty miles higher up in the mountains at Greenbrier River.

I will now tell you something of our adventures since we came to this place on the 11th. We were ordered to attack a strong post fortified by the enemy on the top of Cheat Mountain. We started about eleven o'clock at night and reached the intended battlefield at about eight o'clock in the morning. Our advance guard was some distance ahead and had gotten between the enemy's picket guard and their camp when they commenced firing upon our guard. The firing did not last long and our men proved to be much better shots than the enemy. We killed eight of the Yankees dead and wounded a single man on our side though the bullets whistled all around our devoted heads.

It was uncommon bad weather all the time we were in the mountains. We slept on the ground for four nights with only one blanket apiece, and what was the worst thing that happened to me was that in going up the mountains I lost one of my shoes in the mud and it was so dark that I could not find it and then of course I had to carry one until I came back to camp. You must wonder at soldiers having to do without shoes and blankets sometimes. I believe men can stand most anything after they get used to it. The hardest part is getting used to it.

Miss Bettie, don't you think that I will know how to appreciate a comfortable home with its luxuries after my enlistment is out? I think I will at any rate. There is a current report in camp that we will be ordered back to Georgia soon. I cannot say that I am glad of it as I had much rather stay in Virginia until my enlistment is out than go to Georgia and be there through the expiration of it!

There is a good deal of sickness in camp here sometimes. There are seven or eight deaths a day in the 12th Georgia Regiment and in the 8th Arkansas Regiment there have been several cases of typhus fever. Our regiment is generally the healthiest of them all. I heard a few days since that Captain Thornton's company had been ordered to Manassas. If he has, Hyten will have the pleasure of seeing a hard battle as it is generally thought there will certainly be a great battle fought very soon at or near Washington.

I wish that it would come off soon, as I believe it would have a considerable influence upon the general state of things in other countries; I see that the Spanish Government has since saluted the flag of our Confederacy as another power in existence and if England and France would acknowledge its supremacy we would then have a still stronger faith in foreign powers as an assurance of our soon becoming one of the great nations of the earth but they are holding back to see the issue of another large battle to decide on which side to uphold; if we should be successful, then we will have gained their confidence and I am almost certain that the southerners will always prove so when they are met by their equals and upon fair grounds. I will now drop such foreign subjects and talk about home! . . .

I will now bid you farewell for the present, hoping you all the happiness that this cold world can give and at last a happy one beyond the skies, where the wicked cease from troubling and the weary are at rest.

Yours most affectionately,
JOHN HOLLOWAY

— ★ —

Theodore Compass served as a first sergeant with the 20th Massa-chusetts Volunteer Infantry. The following letter was written eleven days after the Battle of Balls Bluff, near Leesburg, Virginia. The Federal forces, which totaled 1,700 men, suffered a costly defeat—49 killed, 158 wounded, and 714 missing.

Benton
1 Nov. 1861

FRIEND CUTTLE,

It was my intention to write to you ever since our fight, but knowing the paper account was long before in your hands, I intended to wait and see whether the account is given rightly, and if so, all I could say, it was so—but I have not seen a single account that gives the 20th Regiment credit for what they did, therefore my report.

On Sunday afternoon at 2 o'clock, the long roll sounded in our camp, followed up by distant drums from all sides. In five minutes all and everything was ready and only waiting for the order march, but to our astonishment only five companies received the order march, commanded by our Colonel—as they left, I felt perplexed, but our Captain was the Officer of the day and our company had to remain and guard the camp.

The 15th Mass., Colonel Baker's California, the New York Tammany Regiment [42nd New York Volunteer Infantry] accompanied our regiment, and they started for the Virginia side. They crossed the Potomac in three boats, each large enough to hold about 50 to 75 men. They landed on an island this side from the Virginia side, about 15 to 20 rods from the Virginia Shore. This was done in the night.

At about 1 o'clock A.M. the 15th Mass. left the island and landed in Virginia, covered by 3 cannons, which they had planted on the island. As soon as they landed, the 20th Mass. started, then the cannons, then Baker's, then the Tammany Regiment, till they all got over safe and no shots fired at them. While this transpired all in the dark, three more companies of the 20th, who were on picket guard four miles above the shore, were ordered to march double quick to this island and to hold this island as a reserve, which was done all in due time.

At about daybreak Monday morning, the 15th Mass.—who were ahead—were fired upon. They returned the fire and drove the enemy's pickets. To show you exactly how the land was, I'll give you a sketch and you will see at once how unfavorable the position was for our troops. Soon after this, however, the 15th Mass. came back from the woods, followed by about 3,000 rebels, who fired upon them volley after volley.

As soon as they came near enough, our three guns opened upon them, which silenced their firing. Our troops laid down and rested themselves for about a couple of hours, without a single shot being fired. These troops were only intended as a feint, as the real crossing was going on at Edwards Ferry 12 hours later.

General Stone never expected these troops would have to fight

Post Office Headquarters, Army of the Potomac, Falmouth, Virginia

at all, as he only knew of two regiments being there, and knew our boys could beat that number. Instead of that, they had at least from 7,000 to 10,000 men there, all concealed in these woods; at about noon the rebels commenced again to fire from the woods all around on this plain, where our troops were sitting, playing together. Our troops formed a battle line and commenced firing upon them as fast as they could. Our cannon replied also with vigor, but we had the disadvantage, they could see us plain, and we could not [see them]. Behind every tree, on the top of trees, they were concealed and picked our men, all our men on our batteries were picked off in one hour.

Colonel Lee himself loaded one gun 3 times after that, but all in vain. Col. Baker called then on our men to charge. The 15th and 20th Mass. led the charge twice, the California on the rear; the Tammany did not charge, and lost their reputation amongst our boys. Still, they say they obeyed orders from their Colonel, but what everybody says must be considered. I have talked to over 200 men, and they all say the Tammany ran back to their boats before the order came and did not support the advance at all.

Col. Baker and Captain Schmidt of the 20th fell on first charge; a great struggle ensued for their bodies then and the bayonet alone done the work. Our boys fought like tigers, one man in our hospital got three bayonet thrusts in him, but still he helped carry Col. Baker's body back. While this was going on for hours and our boys expecting assistance from the Maryland Tide every moment, no troops could come over; the three boats they had were filled with wounded, who were crossed over to the island by the Tammany men.

Our ranks grew thinner all the time. Still the rebels never came out of their woods. They fired volley after volley and only retreated when our boys charged upon them, but many fell at every charge. At last the order came to retreat. The 15th and 20th covered the retreat. Many swam the river. One boat load sunk with about 75 men in it. The 15th Mass. threw one of our cannons over the bank in the river, while the 20th spiked the other. The other gun could not be taken away.

After the Mass. men fled the steep hill to cross the river, the rebels advanced and fired from the top of the bank upon the swimming men. The next move was that our three companies who were left on the island crossed over in the morning on Tuesday, with a flag of truce, to bury the dead—they buried 85 men, and found the rebels in full force over there.

They say the rebels own up that our Mass. men fought bravely, but said that three times that number could not have carried the day; their position was impregnable and they have taken many prisoners and many arms, but own they lost 280 men; our dead were stripped; their boots, their coats, their money—all were taken from them, and our men said, even their buttons were cut from old coats. Some of our men had twenty to thirty dollars with them, but not a cent was with them when [they were] buried. Our loss is heavier than even the 15th, we sent 300 men to fight, and only 157 returned, out of 24 commissioned officers only 11 returned.

On Tuesday night, the order came for the remainder of our regiment to cross into Virginia. We crossed in the night, and with us crossed thousands of soldiers in large scows, all night. We crossed at Edwards Ferry—the Michigan boys were used to working the boats. The 19th Mass., the remainder of the 20th, and the Minnesota Regiment of Bull Run fame formed the advance, then came our Rhode Island Batteries. It grew daylight by that time.

General Lander received us at the other side, with his cavalry regiment, who came from another ferry, accompanied by the Mass. Sharpshooters, who are very efficient. He looked careworn and almost shed tears. When he saw the remainder of our regiment, he addressed us, cheered us up, and said, "If I would have been with you, I would have found a way out of a field before entering it."

He gave our Captain, who was senior captain of the regiment, the preference of position, who took the advanced post guarding our Mass. Sharpshooters, engaged already in digging rifle pots. By this time the weather became bad and a high wind set in. No boats could cross, and the whole column of Banks' army, who were lined all along the Maryland side and tried in all ways to get over, found the current and wind too strong to cross.

We had 7000 men with us, and General Lander promised our regiment to lead us to Leesburg that day, but he did not foresee that Bank's army could not cross. Our position became dangerous. We knew they had considerable many men at Leesburg—their pickets were clearly seen by us, and the cars going to Leesburg was heard plainly by us, all day. They were receiving reinforcements all the time, and we could get none till the current and tide changed.

As we were talking together in this way, a volley came at us from the front, and a regiment clearly showed itself coming upon us, with flags flying. Our batteries from the Maryland side, as also from the Virginia side, threw their shells right in the midst of them, before we could fire, and we were ordered back, thinking they would follow us, which General Lander expected, and to have a good fight on an open field. But they retreated, carrying their dead with them; from that time till late in the evening, pickets from both sides were shot at constantly.

Here let me praise my Mass. Sharpshooters. They fired accurately a mile, hardly ever missing and killing many. We could see them fall. They have telescopes attached to their guns, which weigh on an average 30 pounds. We lost two men and three wounded that day. General Lander was shot at, but only received a flesh wound on the leg.

The Mississippi Sharpshooters opposed our Mass. men. At about 2 o'clock Wednesday night, our regiment was called up, and to my astonishment, nearly all our troops were out of sight. We were taken to the Potomac again and crossed over to the Maryland side. General McClellan was there himself and by his orders all troops were safely brought back on the Maryland side, without losing a man, nor anybody knowing anything of it till he was called upon. No drum was beat, and the utmost silence prevailed. The locomotive and cars were heard from Leesburg all night, and a large force was there to attack us in the morning. If it had not been for the high wind and water, the expedition would have been successful and Leesburg would have been ours, but Banks' division was going to support Stone's and Baker's, and as they failed to cross, the expedition failed . . .

I will not be selfish, but still some may call me so, if I relate an incident to you, concerning myself. When our regiment was fired upon, and we retreated to our main force, all our overcoats and blankets were left at a haystack near us. It was growing dark and very cold. I went to our Captain and asked him whether he gave me leave to go to that haystack and get some of those coats. He said "No." I went to our Lt. Col., who arrived soon after, and asked him. He said it was dangerous to go outside of our pickets, but if I wanted to go at my own risk, I could.

I went and went alone, my gun was my only companion; it was a quarter of a mile distant, still right in sight. I succeeded in bringing as many overcoats back with me as I could carry. I called then for volunteers to go with me again and—with 6 men—I went seven times back and forward till I got everything safely back. . . .

Yours,
TH. COMPASS

Theodore Compass was killed in action at Glendale, Virginia, on June 30, 1862.

— ★ —

The following letters were written by James Holloway, who served as a surgeon with the 18th Mississippi Volunteer Infantry.

Leesburg
November 2, 1861

MY DEAREST WIFE:

I wrote you two or three days ago by Sergeant Major Stewart enclosing a fifty dollar bill, but from some cause he has been detained and will not leave for Jackson for some days. I left the letter in his hands because it will probably be safer and reach you more directly. If you need any more money, let me know and you will have it. I supposed that you possibly had enough clothing except calicos for the winter and this will go to giving you an abundance. I intend that my expenses hereafter shall not be so heavy.

Last night we were ordered to move immediately—[as] the enemy were advancing and would likely cut us off from the main force—but it commenced raining and continued pouring so hard during the night that the move was almost impossible. The men were packed up with tents struck and in the wagons, so most of them had to make the best of the night in a drenching rain—it is still raining and blowing a gale—which so long as it lasts will prevent the men from crossing the Potomac. They have an idea of having a swollen river between them and a haven of safety.

Our position is extremely dangerous. We have the advance column on the left flank, are fifteen miles from reinforcements and encamped in a horseshoe by the Potomac—the enemy in low water could approach us by four different directions. They have the men, thirty thousand of them, in the opposite side from Harper's Ferry down to Dranesville, and why they do not attack by these different routes is a matter of astonishment to every thinking man. They may do so yet, and fear of it keeps us constantly on the alert, packed up and ready to move at a moment's warning.

It is not at all pleasant to be so situated. One cannot lay down to rest at night with the expectation of remaining undisturbed. We can make no calculation for the next day. A great many of my wounded are still here, not able to move but doing well—I do hope we will get them all back safely before the place is occupied by the enemy.

I have done more work since the fight than all the rest of the surgeons. Dr. Gilmore and myself in fact have to do it all now. I only visit the cases and direct as to how their wounds should be dressed. I leave it for the other doctors to do the dirty work. My cases have been very interesting. I have derived more benefit from this fight than one could generally expect, for most of the cases have come under my notice after operation—generally they are sent back into the interior to be attended by those who have no particular interest in their recovery.

My success in operating has encouraged [me] more than all the practice I've had and it in some degree softens the pangs of absence from my family and the ingratitude of those whom I've been a friend to. I will tell you another thing, wife—I have not taken but one or two drinks since the fight. My head has been all the time cool and I intend it shall continue to be so, and now don't think from this that previously I had been drinking hard—for over two months I have been sleeping at Mrs. Orr's and they will testify to the regularity of my habits. . . .

My love to all the little ones and expect to hear from me again soon. I'll try and be with you at Christmas.

Your affectionate husband,
J. M. HOLLOWAY

December 25, 1861, 3:00 A.M.
Mississippi Hospital
[Near Dranesville, Va.]

MY DEAREST WIFE AND BABIES:

A healthy Christmas to you all and to father and son and the rest. I can't say a happy one (though I wish it), for happiness is not ours until we all meet after the war. We may be joyous and gay for the season but that joyousness and gaiety is mingled with concern and apprehension for the condition of our beloved country—for our absent loved ones, for our poverty, for the doubt as to the truthfulness of English news, for the fear that "old Abe" and cabinet will not "stand up to the test," etc., etc.

I went to sleep last night, my dear wife, at dark (you remember how sleepy I used to be at dark) and at twelve woke up and could not find sleep again. Jake has made me a big fire, fixed my bath and gone to sleep again. . . .

You have no idea how lonesome I feel on this day. It's the first time in my life that I'm away from loved ones at home. Sam is in the regiment and doubtless feels like myself, or will when he wakes up in the morning. I presume you are in New Orleans and in a few hours the house will be all astir—the children crazy over their stockings. Were I there, I'd fill them up to the brim with bon-bons—I'd make them think that for one day plenty abounded, that no war existed, and that each was a king or queen. The delusion should last until they're old enough to appreciate and take part in the holy crusade.

Our men are ordered into winter quarters. There has been a disastrous fight or skirmish at Dranesville within the last eight days, a foraging expedition under command of General Stuart. You have possibly seen glowing accounts of it in the papers as having been a victory for our side. Don't believe a word of it— for I happen to know that we were as badly whipped as ever. They surprised Stuart in a lane between high fences with grape and musketry, and the confusion was so great that the Kentucky and North Carolina regiments fired deadly fire into each other. This is an honest confession and a true one. It will teach us a lesson to be more careful.

If the Yankees had been brave, we would have met with a severe loss, but such was their cupidity that instead of following up their advantage they beat a hasty retreat. We sent our foraging wagons and the less we say about the fight the better for us. Won't the Northern papers teem with accounts of the fight! We have an epidemic in the hospital at present and will break up and move to Leesburg again.

My only real bad luck since I became a surgeon has been here. Have lost as high as six in one day with congestive fever coming on in the midst of typhoid fever and pneumonia. I have done my duty and don't blame myself for the mortality.

Have six invitations to Christmas dinner today. Jake leaves for town after breakfast and I'll go too probably, don't know where I'll be tonight. You know how much I like eggnog. I'll write before New Year. My best love to yourself and babies, and presuming that you are in New Orleans I send my best love to father and the children. Hoping you have written me today, I am still your devoted husband.

JAMES M. HOLLOWAY

— ★ —

At the time of writing, Oliver Wilcox Norton was serving as a private with the 83rd Pennsylvania Volunteer Infantry. He later became first lieutenant with the 8th United States Colored Troops.

Camp Porter, Va.
Jan. 28, 1862

DEAR COUSIN L.:

I returned from the picket lines yesterday and found your pleasant letter of the 24th awaiting me. If you were in Camp Porter about 5 P.M. when that plastic individual that the boys call "Putty" arrives with the daily mail, and could see the interest with which his proceedings are watched as he distributes the spoils, your fears of burdening me with an extensive correspondence would soon vanish.

I never thought so much of letters as I have since I have been here. The monotony of camp life would be almost intolerable were it not for these friendly letters. We do not expect much news, but they are like the delightful small talk that does so much to make time pass agreeably in society.

The worst feature of camp life is its influence upon the mind and character. The physical discomfort, hard fare, etc., I can endure very well, but I sometimes shrink from the moral or immoral influences that cluster round the soldier. The severe physical exercise is so fatiguing that but little disposition is felt to exercise the mind in anything that is beneficial. Everything that requires close or long continued thought is excluded from the common soldier's tent and he usually settles down to the conviction that all he needs is enough to keep himself posted in the news of the day and a little light reading. Thus the stronger mental faculties are unused, and of course they rust.

Another evil is the absence of all female society. The roughest characters are always to be found in the army, and, the restraint of home and more refined friends removed, those who are better disposed are exposed to the influence of such characters without remedy. Our associations go far to mold our characters, and as a constant dripping wears away the stone, this influence must have its effect. The cultivation of the finer feelings of the heart is neglected, and they too are not developed. The pure and elevating influence of music is lost. I am passionately fond of music (although a poor singer) and I miss this as much as any one thing. The music of the field is the fife and drum or the brass band, and the songs sung in camp are not at all remarkable for beauty or purity.

With all these drawbacks, there are many pleasant times in the soldier's life. One of these is when he is the recipient of letters like yours; they speak to him in louder tones than those of the press or pulpit and bid him resist these evil influences and keep himself pure; they atone in a measure for the absence of friends and remind us that they are watching to see if we do our duty, and feel interested in our welfare. You need never fear burdening me with letters.

I fear that, if all the guide you had was my most graphic description of myself, I might pass you in Broadway ten times a day

Soldiers with the 164th New York Infantry playing chess in camp

without recognition. I might say, however, that I am of the "tall and slender" order. Five feet nine is about my height, and one hundred and thirty-five pounds my weight. I am set down in the army description book as having brown hair and blue eyes, and, I might add, of very ordinary appearance.

I see you are a thorough abolitionist. I am glad of it. I thought I hated slavery as much as possible before I came here, but here, where I can see some of its workings, I am more than ever convinced of the cruelty and inhumanity of the system. It has not one redeeming feature. I was on picket duty last Sunday and some seven of us went out a mile or so beyond the lines on a little scouting party. I stopped at a little cabin near the Leesburg turnpike to get some dinner. I found an intelligent and cleanly mulatto woman in the house, surrounded by quite a number of bright little children. She promised me the best she had, and while she was preparing some hoecake and bacon, I entered into conversation with her.

She was quite communicative. She was a slave, she said, so was her husband and the children. Her master was in the rebel army and she was left in charge of her mistress, who lived in a respectable house across the way. Her husband had been taken about a month ago to work on the fortifications at Leesburg. He had, at first, refused to go with his master and was most brutally beaten. She showed me the post where he was tied up and told the story with an earnestness that nothing but actual experience can give.

I talked long with her and told her I hoped this war would result in giving her and all of her class their freedom. "I hope so, Massa," said she, "but I dunno, I dunno." I had a little Sunday-school paper that I took out with me from camp. I read some of the stories to the children and gave them the paper. How their eyes sparkled as they saw the pictures! But the reading was Greek to them. The mother said, "I would study ten years if I could read like you, Massa. A black woman taught me some letters, but Massa Blaisdell took my spellin' book away and whipped me and he said 'larnin wasn't for niggers.' " This is "the land of the free and the home of the brave."

We are still at Hall's Hill, and as far as I can see likely to stay here. No movement can be made while the roads are such a state. . . .

— ★ —

In August 1861, General Alpheus Williams of Detroit, Michigan, was appointed a brigadier general of United States Volunteers. In October, he was assigned to the newly created Army of the Potomac, stationed in the vicinity of Harpers Ferry, West Virginia. Until the close of the war he was in constant service, and in command of several divisions and Army corps.

[February 1862]

MY DEAR LEW:

Sitting in your parlor or resting quietly snug in your warm bed, it may seem very easy to talk of winter campaigns and to call out "Onward" in mid-winter. But if you will come down to these snow-clad hills and take one midnight's round to my outposts, see poor devils in rotten tents not fit for summer, talk to the sentinel on his two hours' round without fire, see the damnable roads, figure up how much provisions it takes to feed a few thousand daily, hear the *cries* not of men only but of half-frozen animals (mules and horses) of which I have upwards of 800—half frozen and half killed by work—witness the effort it takes to get forage, which I buy from twenty to thirty miles away, to transport subsistence stores thirty miles away, you will be satisfied that in winter months a stationary force has about all it can do to subsist itself, especially in the rain, snow, and mud we have had for the last twenty days.

For while it freezes hard at night, it thaws in the valleys by day, or it snows on the hills and rains in the valleys. Altogether I have never seen such cursed weather and such devilish roads.

I should like to photograph for you one day's work here. I have five regiments of infantry, six pieces of artillery, and two compa-

GENERAL ALPHEUS WILLIAMS

nies of horses. In the morning begin the reports, and with them the requisitions for things wanted. I have been four months trying to get things absolutely necessary for comfort. I have had requisitions for thousands of shoes and have received but five hundred for two months. I have hundreds of men nearly shoeless. But for supplies from the states [they] would have been absolutely barefooted. I had men who could not march from Frederick for want of shoes! I have written and telegraphed, cursed and swore, and pleaded and begged, and in return have had promises that they should be sent forthwith. But they came not. Just fancy in this age soldiers left without shoes in this war for the Union—and that in mid-winter and in a campaign!

Again, but two of my regiments have Sibley tents, the only ones you can live in in winter, because [they are] the only ones in which you can use a stove. One of the other regiments has common wedge tents used all through the three months' campaign and literally in shreds. One other has almost equally bad—wholly unfit for this season. These regiments have hutted themselves up to our march here. . . . Now it cannot be done. I have for months had the promise of Sibley tents but they come not!

I made requisition for bugles for skirmishing drill four months ago. They are needed for the efficiency of my command. I have had the promise of them fifty times, but do not get them.

Same of axes and entrenching tools—same for everything. It takes months to have a requisition filled, yet I see the papers every now and then boast of how excellently our troops are provided. It is all a sham, except in rations. We have never wanted for an abundance to eat. It is the only department that is provided, or if provided makes its regular issues. In all other things the troops are woefully neglected. . . .

But if we have suffered some, Jackson's command has suffered more. We have reliable information that he sent back over twelve hundred frozen and sick men during the few days he lay opposite. People who came over yesterday say the sick and disabled fill every house from Bath to Winchester and that many amputations have taken place from frostbites. His whole command was exposed to a heavy snow-storm, followed by intense cold. I see the Dixie papers confirm the reports of his disasters. He lost a good many men, too, from our Parrott guns, which were admirably served, every shot landing plump into his batteries, upsetting his guns, killing his horses, and throwing his men into confusion. A loyal man who was on that side told me that men were killed by some of the last shots thrown purposely high, at least two miles from the river bank.

On their side, the firing was miserable. They literally did no damage to the town, even though some shots passed through roofs of houses and some shells exploded in the streets. Not a person was wounded. Most of their shot fell short or passed high over the town into the hills beyond. . . .

Love to all,
A.S.W.

— ★ —

David Ash served with Company B, 37th Illinois Volunteer Infantry. His letter was written three days after the Federal victory at the Battle of Pea Ridge, Arkansas.

Sugar Creek, Arkansas
March 11, 1862

DEAREST ELIZA:

I seat myself down to let you know that I still am alive and enjoying good health. Well, Eliza, I received a letter from you a few days ago that had been on the way a long time. But I was glad to hear from you at any time.

I must try to tell you what we have been doing. Price and McCullough attacked General Sigel on the 6th. He retreated back to our camp, but kept firing into them all the way on the morning of the 7th. Our division was called on to rally and be on hand at any time. We kept moving from one point to another until two o'clock P.M., and we found where they were in the brush around.

Our brigade, the 37th and 39th Illinois regiments, formed a line of battle and marched into the butternuts. We marched up in front of them within about a hundred yards, and firing commenced on both sides. We all dropped down in the brush and fired and loaded. Jim Lee dropped dead at my feet by a shot from one of Company A, which was on our right. I saw the ball strike him on the back part of the head. He never moved a muscle.

The balls flew thick and fast. They cut the brush all around my head, but fortunately none hit me. We all fell back a few rods and loaded and went up on to them again. We fired into them again and they returned the fire. There were four regiments of them engaged at that time and only two of us. They had a good many Indians, one Brag, Louisiana regiment, and I don't know where the rest are from. . . .

There was a buckshot hit me in the shoulder, just merely going through my clothes, and made a little red spot. The ball had no force at all. It might have hit something before it hit me. I fired eight shots into them the first day, but it was not all over yet.

The morning of the 8th, we were rallied out before sun-up and went about a mile and formed a line of battle along a fence. Three of our company were positioned a few yards to the right along a fence, and our battery began to play upon them. There is two batteries firing at them but they have the best position and we moved back a short distance and formed again. They put balls around us with their battery until we moved, cutting trees off all around us. A ball hit one of our horses on the hind leg and cut it off but our men planted their battery again and began to fire into them, and in a short time they had silenced their battery entirely. They fired over us every time after we moved and did not hurt a man.

Five regiments then formed a line and commenced to advance on to them. We came on to them in about a mile [and] found them in the brush again. We opened on to them again and they ran like whiteheads. But we stopped some of them in the brush for good, they were thick laying dead as they fell. There was quite a lot of them killed. There was a flag taken. It was a beautiful one. Our

Lafayette flag waved triumphantly that day. The Illinois 59th had no flag and Colonel White asked Captain Dick for it and he let him have it. It looked grand floating after the enemy, they brought it back honorable.

After we chased them clear out of the brush, we made a halt to rest and wait for orders. As we were very tired, I went all·through the brush to see what had been done. I found any amount of dead secesh [secessionists, i.e., Confederate soldiers] and none of our men at all. I guess our division lost two or three men on the 8th and two or three wounded. They wound a great many more in proportion to what they kill than we do, for their guns are not so good—they have a great many shotguns and small rifles. Their surgeons don't have many of our balls to pick out, for they generally go through.

It is the hardest sight a person could behold to see the dead lying round after they bring [them] in. They lay them in a pile until they get time to bury them. There was twenty-one killed out of our regiment [and] one hundred and nineteen wounded. Albert Hilliard was laying alongside of me when he was shot, says he, "Oh Dave, I am shot." It was the hardest thing I have done for some time to call the roll the first time after the battle, so many of our boys wounded and one killed. But Eliza, I don't know whether it is over yet or not, they've gone back a piece. It may be they are getting a good ready to come at us again. But I guess we can do the same thing for them every time.

I must close, for my paper has almost run out. If I am spared, I will write to you the first chance I have to send a letter. Dear faithful girl, I bid you goodbye for present. May the richest of heaven's blessings be yours. Be a good girl and remember me.

D. L. Ash

— ★ —

At the time of writing, Aden Cavins was serving as a captain with Company E, 59th Indiana Volunteer Infantry. The follow-*

*Other letters by Aden Cavins appear on pages 184 and 204.

ing letter to his wife is extracted from an anthology that Colonel Cavins published after the war.

Steamer *Nebraska*
Tennessee River
April 21, 1862

I wrote you yesterday while landed at Fort Massac below Paducah [Kentucky]. We are now steaming up the river rapidly. At daylight this morning we passed Fort Henry, which you will remember is twelve miles from Fort Donaldson. We will arrive at Pittsburg Landing about ten o'clock tonight and will not embark until morning. The Tennessee river is a beautiful stream, but there is not much improvement on its banks. The country is partly low, and part beautiful, rolling hills. The whole country is suggestive of poetry and fiction.

I had nothing to write you but not being otherwise engaged I write because it is pleasant to do so to you and because it will also afford you pleasure. You must not be uneasy about me, for it would be a bloody fight indeed for one-tenth of my men to be killed and one-fifth wounded, so that though none are safe in battle, yet the chances are more in favor than against one. You will find consolation in the reflection that none die before their time comes and that there is a Providence that shapes and controls the destiny of the living and the dead.

When in company with some persons of education, you have heard us speak of the Differentials, or vanishing quantities employed in the higher mathematics. These are quantities infinitely small, but still are quantities. Human life seems to me when compared to the infinite future much like one of these Differentials. It is small, very small. It is a short dream filled up with episodes of light and shade, happiness and sadness.

You remember the beautiful tradition of some of the old Jewish Rabbis. It was that little angels were born every morning of the beautiful streams that go running over the flowers of Paradise, their life was sweet music for one day, then they died and subsided in the waters among the flowers that gave them birth. Forgetfulness soon came over their sweet roseate and musical life, and they are remembered no more forever. Such is that part of our existence called human life. We are born, live but a day, are placed in the temple of "silence and reconciliation" where lie buried the strife and fierce contentions of life. Soon the veil of oblivion is spread over all and there remains no heart beat to commemorate the departed.

I seldom indulge in fancies but merely have deviated from my usual habit on account of the poverty of news, and only do it in this case in view of the freedom I claim in writing to you in any way that judgment or humor may dictate. You are aware that at times a storm of fancies sweep across my mind. I have suppressed them through life, but they will loom up occasionally through the matter-of-fact surface that I have cultivated.

— ★ —

Amos Steere served as a private with the 25th Massachusetts Volunteer Infantry. Private Steere was a member of the regimental band and also acted as a stretcher bearer in combat.

New Bern, N.C.
May 2nd, 1862

DEAR SISTER LUCY:

. . . In one of your letters written to me I believe you wrote asking of me to give you some information in regard to a person's feeling when upon the battlefield. I can only speak for one, but have heard the remarks of a great number and their feelings are as different as their minds are at home or upon any subject.

As for my own, when we were marching along (on our march up the river road to New Bern) the next morning (after encamping out all night in the rain without any covering) up the road in front of the enemy's works, I was startled by the sound of a cannon directly ahead of us, the Regt. having just turned in to the right along the woods, we being in the rear of the Regt. They had just got past the turn of the road, which left us in front, then the 27th [regiment], being the next in advance.

The instant I heard the report, whiz and spat came the ball. It struck in the road about ten feet from me, spattering the mud into some of the boys' faces. At that time I thought it best to get out of the range of that gun and acted accordingly. I crossed the road into an open field, with two or three buildings upon it. There we established our hospital, or at least were to do so, but before we had got halfway across, the fire had begun to be terrible. I did not expect to get to the buildings without being hit, but fortunately there was not one of us hurt through the engagement.

After crossing the field and arriving at those houses, we found we were in more danger than before, for we were directly in front of their field pieces. The distance was short of a half mile and only but a trifle farther from their water battery—of which four of their heavy guns could be brought to bear upon us. I believe there was only three or four shots fired from that battery, as they were waiting to get a larger haul but was whipped before they were aware of it. As I said before, when we were at those houses the cannon balls, shells and bullets in abundance were flying all around us.

To add to our misery, one of our gun boats opened fire, intending to throw the shells over in amongst us. One burst in the ground just seven rods from where we stood. The next burst over the house. Then we thought best to make our quarters somewhere else, so we did, but how we got out of it without one of us being wounded is a mystery to me.

I felt the need of religion then if I ever did, and wished that I might be a Christian so that I shall in time of battle and at all other times be prepared to meet my God in peace. I have met with no change of heart as yet, but long for the time to come when it will be as easy for me to do right as it is for me to do wrong. Others say that they had not the least feelings of fear from the beginning and others say that they began to think they were cowards, and others something else.

I think as a general thing those at home that are naturally timid are the ones here that have the least fear. For a sample, I will give Patrick Cronan, Co. E, 25th Mass. [regiment]. He was a sort of street bully as they term it at home and has fought one prize fight here at New Bern. He skulked out of the fight and afterwards was court marshaled and sentenced to wear at guard mounting and through the day a wide board on the back with the word *coward* in capital letters marked on it for five days, then to have his head shaved, the buttons cut from his coat and drummed out of the service. All of that was executed.

Others that it was thought would not fight at all fought the best. . . .

Collecting the remains of the dead at Cold Harbor, Virginia, where battles raged on June 21, 1862, and June 1–3, 1864

I have no particular news to write except our Fort is nearly completed just outside of the city, of which I will give you a plan. Give my love to Mary if you see her, and all the rest of my friends.

From your brother,
AMOS STEERE

— ★ —

The following letters were written by Edwin Fay, who enlisted as a private on April 4, 1862, in a cavalry company known as the Minden Rangers. Private Fay had his first experience under fire while the Rangers were in the vicinity of Corinth, Mississippi.*

Corinth, Miss. May 5, 1862

MY OWN DEAREST:

More than one month has elapsed since I imprinted the farewell kiss upon your lips and this 5th of the month finds me alive and well at Corinth and you need not be surprised that I tell you and that, too, a participant in one battle in behalf of Southern Independence. Yes, the roar of musketry and the booming of cannon are sounds now well known to my ear. I do not wish to give you an exaggerated account and so will simply make a plain statement of facts and you may judge of their significance.

I last wrote you a hastily penned note by Mr. John Vickers of Bienville, on the eve of leaving Grand Junction for, as we supposed, Tuscumbia. After three days hard travelling we reached this place, a distance of only 40 miles. We had to dismount and with ropes pull the wagons up every hill and through every mud hole and some times they were so bad that we had to take out the mules and hitch in the men to get out. That day, the last, I waded in mud knee deep trying to get the wagons through. I was soldier, negro, mule, all three. Wednesday we rested in Corinth and

*Another letter by Edwin Fay appears on page 156.

Thursday morn drew 40 mules from the Quartermaster's department and struck tents, sent them to the railroad for Tuscumbia. Were just getting on our horses when a dispatch came that the train which had gone out had found the enemy about 6 miles and had turned back. Our baggage we had sent from G'd Junction was gone forward and may be for all I know in the hands of the enemy, so I am short of clothing having sent most of it to relieve my horse from the weight. We were then ordered to report to Gen'l [John S.] Marmaduke on the Farmington road 5 miles from here near the advanced outposts of the enemy. We got out after dark and 12 men were detailed to go on picket duty.

The lot fell on Jonah, of course, and we marched over a branch, hitched our horses all saddled and marched on foot across a creek obstructed in every possible manner by fallen timber, burned bridges, torn up crossways to the other side. Dr. Patillo was our officer and the Lieut. of 8th Ark. then on duty took Nat Martin and myself and put us on the very advance. We had not reached our post before snap went a cap at us. I kneeled determined if he fired to try and kill him by his own fire, but the Lieut. said it was his own picket, who was a cowardly fool, which was at once proved by his rushing back on his next man, who fired in reality at him, the ball whistling over our heads through the leaves. We remained almost without breathing for 6 hours constantly on the alert, but not a stick cracked during the time although I found next day we were in 250 yards of a Yankee picket, saw the place where he lay concealed. Also saw a horse that our men killed the eve before. The next day the Col. of the Brigade advanced me some 400 yards farther, further, too, than he was willing to go himself though an aid of Gen'l [William J.] Hardee went with me and looked at the horse which had been killed. Col. Sandidge went through the enemy's pickets somehow or other and went a mile to within sight of their Cavalry camp. He was accompanied by Lieut. Smith of his Co. When he came back he removed the picket who was stationed in my place 300 yds. further back, saying he was liable to be cut off by the enemy's Cavalry.

That evening we returned across the creek, got our horses, went back to our bivouac in an old orchard, slept soundly expecting to be aroused every moment by the firing of our pickets but were not until the next day. The Col. said we might kill some hogs, for the enemy would get them if we didn't. About 12 M. we had killed 6 hogs and were skinning them when our pickets commenced firing rapidly and falling back. I left my pig half skinned and rushed to saddle my horse. We were formed in line of battle and soon received orders to gallop across to another road about 2 miles and try and prevent the enemy from turning our left flank. This we did in haste and found they had got above us already. Capt. Wimberly dispatched a courier "McArthur" (who joined us at Monroe) to Gen'l Marmaduke to announce the discovery. This man we have not seen since or heard of and the probability is that in his haste he galloped right into the jaws of the enemy as he had already occupied the spot where we had left Gen'l Marmaduke an hour before. The Artillery say they saw a courier shot from his horse. We came back and scouted through the woods and to prevent the advance of the Yankee pickets and finally fell in line of battle in an old field.

By this time the enemy much to my surprise had crossed their Artillery over what I deemed an impassable swamp and planted their battery in about 400 yds. of us. Our Infantry, ambushed in the woods, fired a sharp volley on them and according to Gen'l Beauregard's orders fell back. The Artillery opened on the woods and such a roar I never heard in my life before. You have heard and read descriptions of the whizzing of Parrot shells but words cannot describe them. The Minnie balls came like the single buzz of a bumble bee, and you would have been amused to see Capt. Wimberly dodge when one passed near his head. He was in advance of us and we were protected partially by being in a hollow. Our artillery soon opened on our right and I tell you the roar of the duel was terrific. Our guns less in number were heavier than those of the Yankees and were better handled, for I heard the explosion of one of our shells in their battery and such a shriek as rent the air from the Yankees you never heard. Our Artillery filed back after firing some fifty or sixty shots and the Infantry, too, and then we saw a Yankee picket on a fence, within range of my rifle at home, wave his hand and the battery turned loose on us a few shells, but they passed harmlessly over our heads, we being at this time in a hollow. When the Infantry had fallen back some 1/4 of a mile Capt. Wimberly ordered us to the woods and we filed through into an old field 200 yds. in rear of our previous position and formed again. Capt. Wimberly remained up at the woods and a Federal officer rode up in fifty yards of him. Capt. Wimberly looked calmly at him and never once thought of his pistols, till the Federal, spying him, dashed off. Capt. Wimberly is I think a brave cool man but far too forgetful. He kept us in range of that battery 5 minutes too long, tho I admire the spirit he showed on the occasion. He is a brave man sure: too daring sometimes.

We then fell back again and had not left our position 4 minutes when on rising another hill about 500 or 600 yds. there was the enemy's line of battle, 6 regiments strong drawn up on the very ground we had occupied but 4 minutes before. We formed again though the Infantry were double quicking behind us and our Artillery rattling off down the road. The order for us to retreat soon came, and determining to have a good look at the Yankees I rode to the top of the hill to see them. Then bidding them good evening I retired. That night we were kept out scouting, the enemy having followed us within 3 miles of Corinth, and all day yesterday, when it commenced raining and late we came back to camp, tired, wet, worn out and glad to get back safe. Fuller's Co. protected the right flank and one time were in some danger. (I will write between the lines on the first page.) They had one man thrown from his horse who lay in a brier patch and the enemy came all around it and camped in 60 yds. of it. He came off this morning having secreted his gun and accoutrements and passing off as a citizen—George Hearn—your father knows him. A Yankee asked him for fire to light his pipe, he having crawled up to an old house to secrete himself.

Now, dearest, I have given you a succinct account of the whole affair. I was not alarmed in the least till we commenced our headlong gallop reconnoitering. Then I feared we might rush on the enemy before we knew it. During the cannonading I felt just as cool as a cucumber and my only fear was that we should stay till the enemy moved his battery to the top of the hill. I did not like to retreat under fire but would have been willing to charge the battery, for it would have been the safest of the two plans. The boys say my face was spotted white and red but I know how I felt and to you I would express it, tho I have no doubt they were right but I had company in it. All the men acted bravely I think. So much for the battle. The plan of Beauregard is to draw the enemy on to Corinth and I think he will succeed. They are within 3 ms. We had only 3 small Regts. 3 pieces of Artillery and our 2 companies of Cavalry. The enemy had 6 Regts. of Infantry and how much Artillery I don't know—6 pieces at least. I saw no Cavalry. They will record it as a great victory in the *N.Y. Herald* I've no doubt.

Now, dear Mother, do you know that I have had but one letter from you since I left home. Others have had 3 or 4 from their wives. What does it mean, my dearest? I cannot tell you half of what I want to say. Rich is quite sick with flux. I never saw him look half as bad in my life. I hope he won't die, for I assure you I don't know what I should do without him. 'Tis hard enough I assure you to get along with him. You have never read or heard of half of the hardships of camp life. We have a good deal of duty to do, for some will play off on the plea of sickness and that throws it harder on those who are not sick. I cannot do it tho there are many who can. I detest the spirit and it is not those altogether who you would suppose who do it but those who you would think would do their whole duty.

The Conscript Law will let off those who are over 35 yrs. and all are coming home I expect. P. P. Bates is I think tho I don't know when. I am in such utter confusion I can't write what I want. I believe I have told you all about my probably losing my clothing in the car in my valise. One of my overshirts, one Marseilles, and 3 prs. of socks. My needles and thread. My Bible I have with me tho I assure you I have but little time to read it. I have not changed my clothing in two weeks but intend this evening to try and put on some clean ones if I can find a place to wash in. The water around here is only the sweepings of 10,000 camps distilled and would sicken a carrion crow. I drink as little as possible. Oh dirt, dirt I have eaten more than my bushel already and if I ever get back I assure you that I must have things clean in future as an atonement. You must write here your next letter, for I think the probabilities are that we shall remain here till after the great battle which may not come off in a week owing to the heavy rains yesterday and last night. Write me often, my dearest. Take good care of our darlings for my sake, remember what I have told you about them. They must be governed. Write often, dearest. Tell me all matters of little moment and as much "school girl sentimentality" as you call it, as you please. Remember me in your prayers, my own one. I fear I am far from the right road and I fear I will not find it. Kiss our dear ones for their father. Remember me to all my friends. Love to your parents, sisters & brother. I wish I could see you and kiss you.

> Your affectionate husband,
> ED. H. F.

––––––

> Wednesday 14 May 1862
> In Bivouac Van Dorns Hd Qrtrs
> 2 1/2 miles from Corinth
> Near the Enemy

MY OWN DEAREST WIFE:

I wrote you a week ago a long letter which I sent by Mr. W. P. Mabry as also my picture but when I came back from advanced picket I found that Mabry had not got his papers fixed up right and had not gone. He will make one more trial today and I shall send this by him to town and if he does not get off I'll have it put in the Office though I presume that letters will be stopped from leaving here as a battle *is said* to be imminent though I cannot discover that it is any nearer than it was 10 days ago. I presume you have seen in the papers an account of the battle on Friday the 10 inst.* and know much more about it than I do although we were drawn up in battle line all day but got no hand in the fight. It is reported that 800 Yankees were taken prisoners and a Capt. Kitchen of Missouri Cavalry told me that he witnessed a charge of a Regt. of Yankee Cavalry on four pieces of the Washington Artillery and out of 800 troopers only 40 or 50 regained their saddles, the rest being killed or wounded. He saw this with his own eyes, being a support of the Battery.

We have been out on pickett for 6 days, no sleep or rest and are entirely worn out and still the order comes to prepare 3 days' rations for it again after a rest of one night only, though I got sick and came in to camp the day before the rest, so I have had 2 nights' rest. Only 25 or 30 men report fit for duty and the consequence is that we who do go have it all to do. Capt. Wimberly can stand and suffer his men to stand anything rather than protest against the unjust exactions of higher officers. He is not afraid of the enemy but is "mighty afraid" of a rebuke from higher officers. He has not enough confidence in himself from the fact that he does not sufficiently understand Military Law. However you will see him and Dr. [W. C.] Patillo both at home before very long *I think*. The Conscript Law releases both and I think both intend to go. Bert Harper will hire "Cahill" as a substitute and I don't know what we shall do. This is not to go out in the family, at least to the children, for it may prove unfounded. It would not surprise me if our company disbanded entirely.

If I can get a transfer I shall go to Spencer and join his Artillery Co. in case my above predictions prove true. I wish I could be released; I should go as Independent henceforth sure. This living on nothing and not being allowed to go buy for yourself I can't stand. You would have been amused to have seen me living on picket on one biscuit a day and a little piece of *raw* bacon, you

*Fay is referring to the battle at Farmington, Mississippi, that occurred on May 9, 1862 (a Friday), rather than May 10.

would have thought "how are the mighty fallen." I have been right sick for a day or two but feel a great deal better today so I am going out again. Capt. Wimberly does not want anybody to come back even if they are sick and we had some words the other morning about my coming back to camp. He *insinuated that I did not feel very badly* and I have never before failed to perform any duty since I left home. I told him in plain terms what I thought of it. That I should never ask him to go back if I was not really sick. It is a surprising thing to me that the Southern soldiers will fight with so much valor when they are so badly treated. No negro on Red River but has a happy time compared with that of a Confederate soldier. Yet strange to say I am getting more and more used to it, and in fact have got so I like to sleep in the open air. If I come home I think I shall bivouac for the future in your flower yard. News item!!! One of Fuller's men yesterday killed while on picket a Yankee, so he says. I would not be surprised though if he was not a Confederate scout. Fuller's Co. have not established an excellent reputation and I don't know but the same blame attaches to us as we are in the same squadron. Don't mention this as I want nothing to come from me. Don't let my letters be read out anyway.

And now about writing letters. Mail them to me just as often as you can. I shall get them scattering enough anyhow. Don't worry or feel bad if you don't hear from me every week as facilities for mailing letters are not good and sometimes I may be gone on picket 8 or 10 days at a time. If anything happens you will hear from me. I have got all your letters except the one sent by Dr. Harper but when the mail comes and I don't get a letter I feel right bad. Yesterday letters came from Minden as late as May 7 to Webb and David Caufield but none for poor me although I got one from Mother and Spencer but that was not from you by any means. I'll send them by Mabry to you. I burned all your letters before going on picket though I answered all your questions in that letter I believe. I wish you would neglect no opportunity of writing or sending such little things as I have mentioned in my letters. When is Martin Rawls coming? What has become of Johnson? You must write me all the news transpiring in and about Minden.

My Daguerreotype I send you is not like me, for I have fallen off a great deal and then my whiskers cover my face, but it is the best I could do. It cost only $8.oo and I think you will burn it when you see it, at least you ought to. You had better get your father to make a deed to you or me of that 20 acres of land on which our house stands not forgetting to include the strip in front to the branch. This had better be fixed at once as my life as well as your father's is uncertain. I would send you some of the money I have if I had a good opportunity as I have no use for it in camps. If I should get severely wounded I may go to Ala., though I shall send for you at once if I do. I feel in better spirits about a battle and feel as if I should live to see you again, and as Virgil says: "Et forsan haec meminisse juvabit." I wish I knew something to tell you but I assure you if you get the Whig you know more about matters and things than I do.

When you answer my letters read them over and answer my questions, at least make me some reply. It rejoices me to hear such good accounts of Will Ed. and Thornwell. You know that my heart is wrapped up in them. My bible you put up is too large. I can't carry it in my pocket. Send me a small pocket testament. My bible I have to leave in my pack of clothes. Take care of Will Ed. and Thornwell. Teach Will to make letters on a slate preparatory to learning to write. Does Thorn try to talk any? Write me every day a little. You can very easily send two sheets of that thin paper and don't neglect to send a letter once a week anyhow. Tell your father to write to me too, and Lou. I don't care how many letters I get but do how many I write, for facilities are limited I assure you.

I am sitting on my blankets leaning against a tree writing on my knee. I believe I told you the Prattville Dragoons were here but I have not been able to see them yet. Don't know when I will. I must close this as they are starting to the Office. You know that you have my whole heart, dearest. Keep well and don't expose yourself, my dear, for it would hurt me greatly to hear you were sick. Take good care of the children. God bless you, my own dear wife. Kiss all the children for me. Much love to your father & mother. Don't forget to pray for me.

Your affectionate Husband,
ED. H. FAY

Rich has got well again. The Yankees will be badly whipped if they attack us here. They are entrenching 10 miles from here. We won't attack them there. The Tenn. River is going down rapidly. Some things will have to be done soon. Good Bye.

ED

— ★ —

William Nugent* was as a captain with the 28th Mississippi Cavalry. He served on the staff of Brigadier General Samuel Ferguson as assistant adjutant general and later held the same position with Brigadier General William Jackson.

Jackson, Miss.
May 26, 1862

MY DARLING NELLIE,

Judge Yerger has arrived, and although I have forwarded you a letter and a baby dress by Dr. Beden this evening, I have concluded to send along a few lines more. I am in hearing of the voices of fifteen Yankee Prisoners, who are singing "Nellie Gray" and the thoughts suggested by the music are not of the best. These poor deluded victims of a false and aggrandizing policy, far away from home, in the hands of enemies and hedged in by bayonets, are singing to relieve the dull tedium of the day. And while I am listening to them comes obtrusively the thought will I ever be in a like predicament. There is no telling; but my faith in the watch-

---

*Other letters by William Nugent appear on pages 166 and 175.

ful care of a beneficent Providence of the least of whose mercies I am altogether unworthy precludes the possibility of such a thought. I feel as if I will be permitted to return to my own quiet home soon, to caress the dearest idol of my heart, kiss my baby, and eat strawberries from the vines which have yielded you so rich a harvest this spring. As to the peaches, my mouth waters when I think of them, nor do I dare to think the Yankees will have the audacity to destroy my favorite trees. Well, Nell, what are the folks doing with my trees, my *fig* trees, my vines, &c? The grape vines are your Pa's exclusive vanity, and I presume he pays every attention to them.

Jackson is the dullest of towns—I won't dignify it by calling it a city—nothing indicates any activity but those things connected with the war. Generals, Colonels, Captains, and Lieutenants flock in and fill up our Hotels, talk of plans and fighting battles, sieges, gunboats, wars, policy, and scrupulously eke out the last moment of their furloughs away from their commands. I suppose it is a failing of soldiers, who are very similar to school boys during a vacation. But then, at Corinth, we need every officer and every available man. The enemy do not appear to fancy a fight at all. Twice have we offered battle and twice has it been declined. They are concentrating their forces from every available point and preparing for a desperate struggle for Empire. With Beauregard for our Leader, and a good God for Protector, our armies will prevail over theirs, and terrible will be the retribution for all their devastation. Stonewall Jackson has given them a tremendous whipping in Virginia and is driving their routed legions back into Pennsylvania, Beauregard, by the blessing of God, will defeat them at Corinth, Johnston at Richmond and Smith will check their onward career at V.Burg. Altogether we have all to be thankful for to Providence. While we have had reverses, we have had successes. Sleeping upon a fancied security at New Orleans we were suddenly aroused from our fancied security and are being taught the hourly lesson that liberty is the price of ceaseless watchfulness. In fact we needed some lessons that only defeats could teach us. Men learn nothing but by experience, and nations composed of aggregated individuals labor under the same infirmity. Donelson, with all its sad results, taught us the necessity of prompt, united, and vigorous action. This action is being taken and in time, I think, to effect the object of our revolution. In the army there is none of the despondency manifested by the non-combatants at home. The homespun volunteer feels a patriotic ardor which reverses cannot dampen; and the people at home must not complain, if they are called upon to suffer inconveniences. Privations are ennobling to any people if willingly endured for the sake of a public good. Eternal shame should mantle the cheek of the skulking coward, who hopes nothing and does nothing; and while his nerveless arm is not raised in defence of his Country, his croaking voice should be palsied instead of breathing its dolorous accents into the ears of the timid. God bless the women of the South, God bless them! With delicate frames not made to face the pitiless storm of battle, they yet uncomplainingly bear the brunt of privation at home, and hover, like ministering angels, around the couches of those whom war has crushed beneath the iron orbs of his intolerable car. Rallying from the effects of each reverse they gather courage in misfortune, and inspire us with the ardor of their patriotism and the enthusiasm of their souls. If our men of stout frames had but the staunch hearts of our women, Nell, we would indeed be a nation of heroes worthy of the name. We have too long "laid supinely upon our backs and hugged the delusive phantom of hope to our bosoms." We have well nigh suffered ourselves to be defeated. The wonder is that God has blessed us so wonderfully—even beyond our deserts.

I have penned enough. Here's to the health of the "bonnie Ladye" far away and the little baby. How much does she weigh, Nell? I hardly think tho' you had the hardihood to attempt weighing her: the mother is small and I rather suspect the baby is small too—say a three- or four-pound fairy.

Everything is quiet at Vicksburg now. The Gunboats have dropped down the River and the impression prevails that they will land a force of some three or four thousand men and attempt to take the batteries at Vicksburg by a bold push from below. If they do land we will welcome them with bloody hands to hospitable graves. Everything indicates, tho', a speedy termination to the present war. The battle at Corinth will decide the duration of the present contest and if entirely successful there our enemies will be disposed to cease their attempt at our subjugation. They will be satisfied with war and will like to try the cultivation of peaceful pursuits for a time; to which end let us all unitedly lend our prayers and ceaseless efforts.

My health is good now. I have got rid of the Dysentery, I think, and feel very well tonight. Love to all. Kiss Ma and Evie for me and the baby until you are tired. Kiss my picture and imagine it to be me.

May God Almighty have you, my dear Nell, in his watchful care and keeping and keep you secure unto the perfect day is the prayer of

> Yr. devoted husband
> WILL

— ★ —

David Weisiger served as a colonel with the 12th Virginia Volunteer Infantry. His letter was written after the two days' fighting at the Battle of Seven Pines, Virginia, which lasted from May 31–June 1, 1862.

———

> Camp near Richmond
> June 2nd, 1862

MY DARLING WIFE:

I've no doubt, from what I have heard of the rumors in Petersburg, that you are in agony about me. Yesterday I requested Ben Harrison to telegraph you from Richmond that I was safe. Oh! my dearest I have had a very hard time, but the sufferings in the way of hardship is nothing to what I have suffered in mind at seeing some of my best men and brave boys shot down before my face, to say nothing of thinking about your misery on my account. My darling, even upon the battlefield in the thickest part of the action I thought of you and what pain you would suffer if you only knew my position, but my dear one, I've faith in your prayers on my behalf and cannot doubt that I shall pass through unscathed. The prayers of the righteous avail much.

We were in action about half an hour and lost ten men killed, twenty-seven wounded, and seventy-five missing. You just ought to see me, muddy and dirty up to my knees, without a change of clothing as my horse after being shot ran off.

Rest assured that I will always either write or telegraph you if anything should happen. As soon as times get a little quiet I will try and pay you a visit. I must close. Give my love to all the girls.

Your ever devoted husband,

D. A. WEISIGER

— ★ —

Major Benjamin Rober served as a surgeon with the 10th Pennsylvania Reserves. His letter home was written following the first of the Seven Days' Battles, in Oak Grove, Virginia, which lasted from June 25 to July 1, 1862.

Camp on James River
fifteen miles below Richmond
July 6, 1862

MY DEAR WIFE:

You no doubt received my note in pencil, which was simply to let you know that I was safe. This is about the first opportunity I have had to write at any length. I received your last letter yesterday to find that you were entirely in the dark as to our contest. I will not attempt to describe the week of battles, the papers will give you all the information. I wish you would send a copy of the *Inquirer* commencing on the first of July up to the middle of the month.

On Thursday, June 26th, everything was quiet in and about

Mechanicsville. The reserve corps was scattered about in the woods. I had just received the letter with pictures and was showing them to the boys when messengers came flying in every direction. In a few minutes, the artillery opened the ball in our front and in less time than I can tell you on paper our whole force was out on line of battle.

The First Brigade was to our right [and] received the first onslaught, but in less than an hour the whole corps was in action. Our regiment was placed in rifle pits and literally mowed down the enemy as they approached our front. The result was very little loss of life. We only lost eight killed and five wounded; on this day, the battle lasted from 2 o'clock P.M. until 9 o'clock P.M., seven hours' incessant fighting. Our cannon firing sounded as rapid as you could count and the musketry was incessant—resembling thunder.

It is generally conceded that Thursday's fighting was the most desperate of all the battles. The enemy were ten thousand to our eight thousand, which we held by having the good position, plenty of artillery, rifle pits and, last but not least, the men were fresh, anxious and determined. I took my position in the house near, but in a very little time the shells fell so thick around that we vacated and moved into a gully about six hundred yards in the rear of our regiment and about the same distance from Gaston's Battery.

As it happens, we were in the most dangerous position. The shells fired at Gaston's Battery all came rolling around us. But the excitement was so intense that we thought no more of the danger than if they had been snowballs. While dressing the wounded, I became deaf to all sounds except those of solid shot when they strike the ground. They scoot off with a sound similar to pheasant. It is owing to their shape, being long and leaded at one end.

How we escaped is a miracle, yet we did. As it was getting dark, we had to stop operations. We sat enjoying the scene. There was a perfect blaze of lightning from the continuous discharge of cannon. Captain McConnell was wounded back of the neck, but is now nearly well again. The wounded of the other regiments were taken to a house a mile back where we were at work until three o'clock next morning when we retreated in good order about four miles to Gaines' Mill, the enemy following closely in our rear keeping up a continuous fire. We reached the Mill about nine o'clock [and] everybody lay down to get a little sleep, not dreaming of another battle.

But about noon the word came to be ready. In a short time, musket firing was rapid in all directions. Here was the great battle second only to that of the Seven Pines. Division after division of men rolled in, fell back, in again and so it continued until near ten o'clock at night. The surgeons of the Third Brigade, Clark Philips and myself selected a position nearly three-quarters of a mile below the field of battle on low ground and behind a little hill. Dr. Green and others were nearby in a house. While we were busy with the wounded we knew very little about what was going on until all of a sudden there was a tremendous rush around us.

It seemed that the enemy was coming pell mell, but we soon discovered that they were the cowards. A line of cavalry formed in line and drove them back. There they stood like sheep frightened nearly to death, all huddled together. They could not be driven back, yet it stopped others from following. Just at this critical moment the Irish Brigade came up on [the] double quick, cheering most lustily. With the green flag flying, they formed in line not fifty feet from where I was dressing the wounded.

By this time the enemy had pushed forward and were within a quarter of a mile of my depot and as we expected them to fire on the Irish in front of us we concluded to skedaddle. We hurriedly put all our wounded into ambulances and started across the Chickahominy. The Irish however drove them back and held the field long enough for all our troops to come across when the bridge was destroyed. We had to leave about three thousand dead and wounded behind, very few of our regiment.

That night I was up all night dressing wounded. Here we remained until evening, [it] being Saturday, when the whole army commenced retreating. On Sunday about noon we reached White Oak Swamp, everybody exhausted and completely worn out. We halted to rest, but had scarcely time to stretch our weary limbs when a report came that we were surrounded by the enemy. We started again and moved about two miles further when we halted for the night. This night I got a little sleep, not much.

In the morning, the ambulances came along with our wounded. We again commenced dressing them until twelve o'clock, when news came that the rebels were coming on our right. The trains were sent off in a hurry and the troops formed in a line of battle. Dr. Green, Philips and others and myself took a position in the rear about a half a mile in the thick woods. While [we were] sitting waiting for the battle to commence, all of a sudden the shells fairly rained through the woods, cutting off treetops, limbs and all. We left in short order. Father Hunt was with us at the time. As we rode out together, a shell burst immediately over our heads, small pieces striking our horses, but did no damage.

We then took a church nearby. Although the shell fell all about us while [we were] in the church, yet we escaped. This was a terrible battle. The reserve corps were in the midst of it, and many have fallen, but beyond our reach we have to leave them on the field. Captain Adams, one of our best men, and Adjutant Gaithe both fell mortally wounded. Here we worked until two o'clock in the morning. Arms and legs were piled away in one corner of the church—terrible to behold. The medical director detailed a number of single surgeons to remain and attend to our men so that they will still have our surgeons and not be entirely at the mercy of the enemy.

Tuesday morning at two o'clock A.M., the whole army mowed down towards the lines and selected a strong position. The enemy attacked us at nine o'clock. The battle raged all day up to nine o'clock in the evening. In the afternoon, things looked blue enough. The fainthearted declared that we were whipped and kept up a gloomy front. At five o'clock in the evening, both armies became desperate. First they tried to break through our right and were repulsed and then they came down on our left wing and were repulsed. Then, as the last and most desperate of all, they fell on our center with overwhelming force. We had taken nearly all their artillery so they had to depend upon numbers alone, but as they came up in masses our cannon mowed them down like grass.

Our reserve corps was not called up on this day, so we could be spectators. The battlefield was a large open level piece of ground. On this, our whole force—nearly a hundred thousand men—were placed in position and every movement was before us. Artillery, calvary, infantry were stationed so as to be brought into action; as one division retired, another was seen marching up to take their place. At the same time, cannon were firing from every little elevation. The gun boat sent shell after shell into the woods, where the rebels were the thickest, doing great executions for two hours. They would drive our men back a few hundred yards, then we would drive them again. So it seemed to hang as on a thread, but at last our men gave tremendous cheering and firing became less distant and all was over, the rebels were running for dear life—our cannons then sent shell after them for two miles (we had about 1,000 cannons on the field, which would make it very hot as far as they would reach).

This Tuesday night at twelve o'clock, we again started for the river, some seven miles, which we reached by seven o'clock in the morning of Wednesday. It rained all day and the mud became knee deep. The next morning, the enemy again attacked us, but we very soon drove them beyond reach. Friday, Fourth of July, the flags are flying and the music is abundant again. We have not heard the first sound of the drum for two weeks. Everything has been kept quiet and no fires and light at night. At twelve o'clock, a salute was fired in honor of the day by some field pieces. They made a terrible racket. We have lost heavily in killed and wounded in our regiment. . . .

Read the papers and you will get a better idea than I can give you of the different battles. My health is good. I was exhausted from over-exertion, loss of sleep and nothing to eat, yet I stood it better than any of our officers, with one or two exceptions. I am tired of riding and I have been very busy making out reports.

Ever your affectionate husband,
B.R.

— ★ —

When he wrote this letter, Luther Bradley was serving as a lieutenant colonel with the 51st Illinois Volunteer Infantry. By 1864 he had attained the rank of brigadier general.

———

Camp Big Spring
July 17, 1862

MY DEAR BRIEL,

Yours of the Fourth has just reached me by way of Chicago. Your frequent letters are a great comfort to me and I beg you will not weary of writing. . . .

We move from here tomorrow into northern Alabama. I do not know the exact point we occupy, but we are to relieve General Thomas, who joins Buell. Our location will be on the Tennessee River about forty miles from here. . . . I shall write you immediately on my arrival at the new camp, meantime direct to me at Corinth. We are to hold one of the chain of posts established across the country, with little prospect of anything to do for the present. I am told that the guerrilla parties are showing themselves in that neighborhood and I hope it is true. It needs the occasional crack of firearms to steady our nerves.

I have just read in the *New York Tribune* an article on the "unhonored brave who die on our picket." It is so true of our own experiences in the swamps in front of Corinth at the Tuscumbia, and at Twenty Miles Creek, that I send it to you. All he says of the dangers and toils of picket duty are literally true. In face of the enemy watching a chance to strike, it requires the most sleepless, vigilant and often the most stubborn courage. The pickets are the guardians of the army, and the duties are so sacred that sleeping on post is punishable with death.

I shall not soon forget the last day I was on, in front of Corinth. I had command of the pickets in front of our lines, consisting of ten companies from the different regiments of the division. It was a dark gloomy day and it rained heavily nearly the whole twenty-four hours. The picket line was rather more than a mile from our camp and half that distance from the rebel works. I was cautioned

LIEUTENANT
COLONEL LUTHER BRADLEY

by the officer whom I relieved to be careful, for the line was constantly under fire and he had lost an officer and three men. The line lay through a wooded country for a mile and a half, part of it a heavy swamp almost impassable in the storm, and here and there an open field. The rebel pickets were so near that we could see them plainly. Then they dodged from cover to cover. It is very much like Indian fighting. The whole game consists in keeping yourself covered and trying to catch your enemy exposed.

The Videttes* are within sight of each other, and are relieved every two hours from the picket post. If attacked in force, they fall back on the post and the reserves are advanced. On the day I speak of, the rascals seemed particularly alert. We could not show a head without drawing fire. In the afternoon, we noticed them reinforcing, and pushing forward their lines. So we prepared for them and a good chance offering, we opened a cross-fire on three points that had been very troublesome. We got a volley in return and after half an hour drove them from their advanced post carrying three bodies. We got through the day without losing a man, but the next day the rebels got so bold General Stanley sent out a battery and drove them back with grape and canisters. I don't know when I have felt a greater sense of relief than when I marched my men out of that swamp after being twenty-four hours under fire.

Give my best love to dear mother and tell her to keep up good heart for my sake. With love to you all and kind wishes to all friends.

Yours ever,
LUTHER

— ★ —

*A mounted sentry on picket or guard duty.

Captain Charles Bowditch wrote the following letter several months before his enlistment in the 55th Massachusetts Volunteer Infantry.

————

August 5, 1862

DEAR FATHER:

You remember last year when I spoke to you about enlisting, you said that there were so many men ready to go that there was no need of men of education volunteering. It seems to me now that the case has changed, at least in this state, and men are coming in very slowly to the recruiting offices. I think no one will deny that it is the duty of everyone who is not held back by duties or ties which he cannot break to volunteer and set an example for others to follow. Those who have families to support or whose absence would bring distress to many others have some reason for staying at home. But all others ought to go.

Now here I am, of no earthly use in my present position, and having completed, with the exception of one year, my whole college course. There is no doubt that the country wants men, and that, speedily. The example of gentlemen volunteering would be extremely advantageous. The common people, so far from the war as they are here, cannot perhaps understand the necessities of the occasion simply from newspaper addresses and enthusiastic speeches. But if they saw that the time is so threatening as to require gentlemen to enlist they would have an example before their eyes, which their own senses would lead them to follow.

Don't think now that my wish to enlist is caused by any enthusiasm to see service and get a shot at a rebel, for it is far otherwise. Taking my own feelings simply into consideration, I do not think I should care to go. But as I said before, it is everyone's duty to enlist, if he possibly can, and why is it not mine as much as other people's? I have nobody to depend upon me and am not in a position to bring misery on anyone by going. What can be more clearly my duty than to go?

If you are not willing to send your sons, why should others be

CAPTAIN CHARLES BOWDITCH

willing to send theirs? I wish you would consider this seriously and answer as soon as possible.

Your aff. son,
CHARLES

— ⋆ —

James Binford served as a private with Company F, Second Brigade, 21st Virginia Volunteer Infantry. His letter home was written following the Battle of Cedar Mountain, Virginia, on August 9, 1862.

Liberty Mills
August 13, 1862

DEAR CARRIE AND ANNIE:

Thanks to merciful providence, I breathe and have all my limbs. I am uninjured. I am one of the six survivors of Company F. We went into the field with eighteen men and came out with six. Four killed on the field, and eight wounded, two of who have since died.

It was a bloody desperate fight. I was sun stroke, and fell, which was the only thing that saved me, for almost immediately afterwards the enemy outflanked our regiment and completely surrounded it and we were literally butchered. Our regiment suffered more than any two regiments in the field. We repulsed Pope and drove him three miles from the field. I would not be surprised if the few who remained of Company F were allowed to go home awhile, as our Lieutenant wants it disbanded. So I shall come and stay with you a short while, for I long to go to some quiet place, where loved ones of home are, to rest body and mind.

If we are not disbanded, I shall be transferred to cavalry and get, if possible, a short furlough. The smoke of battle seems still around me, and my ears are yet ringing with musketry and cannon and how sweet does the picture of home look through all this. I can see old Ingleside, and quiet and comfort reigning supreme.

I must say, I have had enough of the glory of war. I am sick of seeing dead men and men's limbs torn from their bodies. I feel grateful to God for bringing me through such scenes of death and suffering safe, and am willing to spend the remainder of my time quickly and smartly. When the war ends, if I am alive, no one will return to peaceful avocations more willingly than I.

I wish I could write a letter to Ma, I have not read one of her letters since the Yankees took possession of Portsmouth. Send Sis some word that I am all right. I do not know whether she is in Richmond or Pittsylvania. Give love to Celia and Sallie and affectionate friends, and write soon too.

Affectionate Brother,
JAMES M. BINFORD

— ★ —

Constantine Hege* served as a private with the 48th North Carolina Volunteer Infantry. Private Hege was a conscript and deadly unhappy about it. After being captured by Federal troops in the autumn of 1863, he took the Oath of Allegiance to the Union cause and worked until the end of the war in Bethlehem, Pennsylvania.

———

August 13, 1862

DEAR FATHER:

I now have the opportunity of writing to you this afternoon stating that I am well at present, hoping that you enjoy the same good blessings. We arrived here at Petersburg today about noon and moved to the camp. There is a battle expected here very soon, and they are throwing up breast works here very rapidly. It is supposed that the fight will extend from Richmond to Petersburg.

It fell to my lot to go in Captain Meikels' Company. I there saw very many of my acquaintances which I had not seen for several months. This revived me somewhat, but I'm not satisfied here. I

---

*Another letter by Constantine Hege appears on page 102.

do not like to hear of going to face the cannon and the muskets, and would be very glad if you could hire a substitute in my place because I cannot stand such a life without any enjoyment at all.

I went over to see the flying artillery. There were twelve cannons there, and for a person to see them would make the cold chills run over anyone, I think. Therefore I want you to try to hire a substitute. If you do hire one, get a competent man to bring him to Captain Meikels'. . . .

We left Raleigh last Monday evening about five o'clock P.M. and came on as far as Weldon on Tuesday morning A.M. and stayed there until Wednesday morning about three o'clock and arrived at Petersburg about ten o'clock A.M. and remained there a few moments and then marched out to our camp about three miles east of Petersburg and we have very bad water here. It is said that the Yankees are about twelve miles from here now. I saw about three hundred Yankees from Salisbury [Prison] on their way home at Weldon. I talked with several of them. They seem to be a fine set of men as are anywhere. . . .

So I must close my letter. . . . I remain your dear son until death.

C. A. HEGE

— ★ —

Warren Freeman served as a private with Company A, 13th Massachusetts Volunteer Infantry. Private Freeman's letter, which is extracted from a privately printed anthology that was published in 1871, is an account of the regiment's operations after the Battle of Cedar Mountain and just before the Second Battle of Bull Run.

In Camp Near Warrenton, Va.
August 25, 1862

DEAR FATHER:

You will be perhaps surprised to learn that we are back here, especially as we are under a general who has always been accus-

PRIVATE WARREN FREEMAN

tomed to look on the backs of the rebels; but here we are, en-camped about five miles from the town. We left Cedar Mountain soon after the battle, and marched round the south side of the Rapidan, or Robinson River, I suppose it should be called. It was seven or eight miles. There were graves all along the road where the rebels had buried their dead.

We remained here for a day or two, then changed camp to a level field about three miles to the eastward. Here the recruits from Boston joined us. We remained here one day, then struck our camps in the middle of the afternoon and formed in line, then stacked arms and laid round till eleven o'clock in the night, and then commenced the march; and after proceeding about a mile we halted and lay in the road the rest of the night—it was too cold to sleep. In the morning, we took up the line of march, passing through Culpeper and over the Rappahannock River, making twenty miles, most of the way in quick time and carrying our knapsacks the whole distance; it was very dusty, and gave our raw recruits a foretaste of what is in store for them. . . .

Tuesday August 26 . . . Toward night we packed up in a hurry and went at double-quick across the river and took possession of a knoll near the bridge. Mathews' Battery crossed immediately after the Thirteenth. We threw out two companies of skirmishers on another knoll to the front and right. The Eleventh Pennsylvania crossed after the battery. They took possession of the hill where our skirmishers were; they supported two pieces of the battery, while we supported the other four.

The advance of the rebels could now be seen in the distance. We had the advantage of position, as they would have to advance across an open field to attack us. Two regiments besides the battery were the only troops across the river that night. We sent out four companies of pickets; everything was quiet during the night. The next morning at daylight, the rebel artillery opened on our right, and so after on our right and center.

While the cannonading was going on, I received your letter of the 17th—rather a singular time and place to get news from home.

But those who brought the letters got frightened and ran across the bridge, taking about half the letters with them; I was fortunate to secure mine, though it took a long time to read it, as I had to make my manners to the rebel shell and shot as they came along. The rebel batteries were finally silenced. There were four killed and wounded in Mathews' Battery; and the adjutant of the Eleventh had his horse shot.

During the day, the other two regiments of our brigade crossed the river. At night, it was our turn to go on picket duty. Next day we had to dig trenches on one of the knolls. During the day we got twenty-three head of cattle; they got away from the rebels and came toward our lines. We made a rush, and they made a rush— but we got the cattle.

Towards night, a rainstorm came on, and by the next morning the river had risen to such a degree that we were fearful that the bridge would be carried away. So we all passed to the opposite bank and posted our artillery on the high ground near the river. When the enemy saw we had left the knolls, they advanced to take them. Our artillery played upon them as they advanced to take possession of the first—and were advancing on the second— when some of our guns that were masked poured a terrible fire of grape and canister into their ranks, killing and wounding large numbers, causing them to break ranks and run in all directions. Some of their shot and pieces of railroad iron came fearfully near to our heads, but we had only one man wounded.

We have been within half a mile of Warrenton, and are now within three or four miles of Waterloo; it seems our luck to visit all places twice. We have not had a chance to send off letters for some time, but our band goes home in the morning and will take letters, I presume. I must close; this constant marching tires a fellow so that he does not feel much like writing.

I am in good health. Farewell all.

WARREN

— ★ —

Spencer Glasgow Welch* served as a surgeon in the 13th South Carolina Volunteer Infantry. The following letter was written to his wife a week after the Second Battle of Bull Run.

Ox Hill, Va.
September 3, 1862

DEAREST:

I was in battle at Manassas and made several very narrow escapes. On Monday (September 1), at this place, I came very near being killed; for a bombshell barely did miss me and burst right at me. I stood the late terrible march surprisingly well, but I have learned what hunger and hardships are. I would often lie down at night on the bare ground without a blanket or anything else to cover [myself] with and would wonder what my dear wife would think if she could see me lying there. We have had some dreadful suffering, especially on these forced marches. The fatigue and the pangs of hunger were fearful.

We marched fast all day Monday and all day Tuesday (August 25 and 26) and until late Tuesday night, when we bivouacked in a field of tall grass near Bristow Station. The next morning (Wednesday) we got up before day and marched fast to Manassas Junction, and almost kept up with the cavalry. Before noon we started towards Washington, and after marching three or four miles we marched back to Manassas Junction again and found many prisoners and negroes there, who were all sent away towards Groveton. We stayed there that night, and all the cars and everything were set on fire about the same time. We were very tired, and all day lay down on the ground, but I remained awake for some time watching the fire, which burned fiercely. Thursday morning (28th), we marched nearly to Centreville, and from there towards Groveton, and Ewell's command got into a fight late that afternoon on our right. We remained there and bivouacked in the oak forest where our brigade fought next day.

---

*Another letter by Spencer Glasgow Welch appears on page 169.

Next morning (Friday), we had breakfast, and I ate with Adjutant Goggans. Our command then took position in the woods near the cut of an unfinished railroad and sent out skirmishers, who soon retreated and fell back on the main line. The Yankee line came up quite near and fired into us from our right, and Goggans was shot through the body. I remained some distance in rear of our line and saw Mike Bowers, Dave Suber and two other men bringing someone back on a litter, and I said: "Mike, who is that?" and he said: "Goggans," just as they tumbled him down. I looked at him as he was gasping his last, and he died at once. Then the wounded who could walk began to come back, and those who could not were brought to me on litters. I did all I could for them until the ambulances could carry them to the field infirmary, and this continued until late in the afternoon.

I saw an Irishman from South Carolina bringing a wounded Irishman from Pennsylvania back and at the same time scolding him for fighting us. Colonel McGowan came limping back, shot through the thigh, but he refused to ride, and said: "Take men who are worse hurt than I am."

Shells came over to us occasionally as if thrown at our reserves, and would burst among the men and overhead, but they paid no attention to them and kept very quiet. I did not hear anyone say one word. An occasional spent ball fell near by and one knocked up the dust close to me, but the trees were thick and stopped most of the bullets short of us. The Yankees charged us seven times during the day and were preceded by skirmishers. One ran into the railroad cut and sat down, and Jim Wood shot him dead.

Our brigade was not relieved until about four o'clock. They had been fighting all day and their losses were heavy. I saw General Field, commanding a Virginia brigade, ride in on our left to relieve us, and I then went back to the field infirmary, where I saw large numbers of wounded lying on the ground as thick as a drove of hogs in a lot. They were groaning and crying out with pain, and those shot in the bowels were crying for water. Jake Fellers had his arm amputated without chloroform. I held the artery and Dr. Huot cut if off by candle light.

We did nothing Saturday morning (30th). There were several thousand prisoners nearby, and I went where they were and talked with some of them. Dr. Evans, the brigade surgeon, went to see General Lee, and General Lee told him the battle would begin that morning at about ten o'clock and would cease in about two hours, which occurred exactly as he said. Our brigade was not engaged, and we spent the day sending the wounded to Richmond.

Early Sunday morning (31st), we started away, and I passed by where Goggans' body lay. Near him lay the body of Captain Smith of Spartanburg. Both were greatly swollen and had been robbed of their trousers and shoes by our own soldiers, who were ragged and barefooted, and did it from necessity. We passed on over the battlefield where the dead and wounded Yankees lay. They had fallen between the lines and had remained there without attention since Friday. We marched all day on the road northward and traveled about twelve miles.

The next morning (September 1), we continued our march towards Fairfax Court House, and had a battle late that afternoon at Ox Hill during a violent thunderstorm. Shells were thrown at us, and one struck in the road and burst within three or four feet of me. There were flashes and keen cracks of lightning nearby, and hard showers of rain fell. The Yankees had a strong position on a hill on the right side of the road, but our men left the road and I could see them hurrying up the hill with skirmishers in advance of the line. . . .

The battle continued till night came on and stopped it. We filled the carriage house, barn and stable with our wounded, but I could do little for them. Colonel Edwards was furious, and told me to tell the other doctors, "For God's sake to keep with their command."

The next morning the Yankees were gone. Their General Kearney was killed, and some of their wounded fell into our hands. The two other doctors with our medical supplies did not get there until morning, and many of our wounded died during the night. I found one helpless man lying under a blanket between two men who were dead.

We drew two days' rations of crackers and bacon about ten o'clock, and I ate them all and was still very hungry. I walked over on the hill and saw a few dead Yankees. They had become stiff, and one was lying on his back with an arm held up. . . .

We hope to be able to go on and catch up with the regiment in a day or two. It has gone in the direction of Harpers Ferry.

— ★ —

Henry Pearson, a captain with Company C, 6th New Hampshire Volunteer Infantry, also wrote home to give an account of the Second Battle of Bull Run.

———

Near Washington
Sept. 5, 1862

FRIEND:

Perhaps you would like to know our experience in the late great battles near Manassas. As my account will probably differ from any which you have seen in the newspapers, I will endeavor to speak only of what I saw.

July 28th we slept at Blackburn's Ford. Jackson was supposed to be at Centreville. Friday we marched up to Centreville and finding no enemy there followed down the Warrenton turnpike to Stone Bridge. Some skirmishing occurred near the bridge, but the enemy falling back, we advanced up the turnpike to the old battle ground. Some of the hills where the old battle was fought have been cleared of their woods, and the open country now lies nearly in the shape of a square bounded on three sides, north, west and south by woods. . . .

About two o'clock Friday, [Major General] Heintzelman attacked the enemy in the belt of the woods on the north side of the square. After half an hour's sharp fighting, the rebels were driven from it back into the woods on the west side. Here they made another stand. Kearney's Division and Hooker's Division were repulsed with great slaughter in succession and driven entirely

CAPTAIN HENRY PEARSON

from this part of the field, leaving nearly half their numbers killed or wounded in the hands of the enemy.

It would seem that after the slaughter of two such divisions as Hooker's and Kearney's, General Pope would have sent a larger force into these woods. Instead of this, however, he ordered up our Brigade, the first of Reno's Division, and ordered us to clear the woods in front of us. Our Brigade is composed of three regiments: the 6th New Hampshire, 2nd Maryland and 48th Pennsylvania commanded by Col. Nagle of the 48th, and would number about fifteen hundred fighting men.

We deployed and advanced in line, the 6th on our left. When we arrived near the wood, we halted, took off our knapsacks and my company deployed as skirmishers in front of our regiment. We had not entered the woods more than three or four rods before the muskets began to pop ahead of us and a few bullets to whistle by us. Still the boys did not halt, but pressed forward to get a sight of the rebels. There are no trees in the woods large enough to cover a man, but it is very thick with small white oak. Soon we could see plenty of snuff-colored pants ahead of us not more than seventy-five yards, and the cracking of rifles became general.

As the regiment came up, Company C rallied on the right. We delivered a volley and advanced, loading and firing. The storm of bullets soon became terrible. The rebels fought us every inch of the way. We charged upon them in a sunken road which ran through the woods parallel to our lines and drove them from it. As they were skedaddling from the ditch road, our boys poured in a volley which literally strewed the ground with them. Halting a moment or two long enough to form and pour in a volley or two, we mounted the other side of the ditch and pressed forward. When we had advanced some fifty paces, we could see through the woods into the open fields beyond. The rebel artillery began to play upon our flank, which did us very little damage, however, as the trees were so thick.

Discovering that our regiment was alone and [that] the bullets began to come thick and fast from the rear, the Colonel sent me back to see why the other two regiments did not follow us and to tell them they were firing upon us. As I approached the ditch, I heard loud cheering on the other side and thought that we were about to be supported, but as a number of bullets whizzed by my ears, I quickened my pace to inform them that we were ahead. Mounting the other side of the ditch, the bullets flew by me so thick that I quickly jumped back again.

Peeping up over the bank, I could hardly trust my eyes when I saw yellow legs standing as thick as wheat not more than twenty-five paces from the ditch. I instantly called to the regiment to retreat to the ditch, which was done at a run. Taking a second look to see if I could spot a flag, I saw one, their battle flag, with a red cross worked in it and a swarm of rebels following it at double quick towards our left, as we were now faced, so as to surround us.

The Col., still doubting whether it could be rebels, took our flag and waved it above the ditch. It was instantly riddled with bullets. In the meantime, our boys were peppering them terribly, as nearly every shot told. But as it was evident that we would soon be surrounded and overwhelmed with numbers, and be all killed or captured, the Col. wisely ordered a retreat up the road which led around into the wood from which Heintzelman had driven the enemy at the beginning of the battle.

When the rebels saw us retreating, they pursued us with loud cheering, and in a few moments we were all mixed together. Bayonets and gun stocks were in some cases used, and very few of our men were taken prisoner unless they were first wounded. The 20th Indiana and 2nd New York coming up, we rallied behind them and with tattered colors flying returned to the ground from which we had started. We had twelve out of twenty officers killed or wounded and two hundred and seventeen enlisted men. Co. C lost eighteen men. As the enemy held possession of the field, we do not know what proportion of our wounded died of their wounds. . . .

After fighting until sundown with little better success than we had, the enemy held the field that night. Just at sundown, I saw one of our batteries run down close to the woods and throw shell and canister into them. The rebels made a rush out and captured one of their pieces. I have since heard that it was the New Hampshire Battery. We slept that night on the ground strewed with bones of horses and men that fell in the First Battle of Bull Run.

Saturday, August 30th, not much fighting occurred in the forenoon nor before two or three o'clock in the afternoon. Troops were marching and countermarching all the forenoon and taking up positions. This afternoon our brigade was held among the reserves near the center. Here at the top of a hill where I could overlook the whole country, I sat all the afternoon watching the progress of the battle. About three o'clock, our lines of attack facing towards the west advanced into the woods and attacked the enemy. Our artillery, except an advanced battery on the left, could not play upon the enemy on account of the situation of the ground and the woods.

For about an hour there was a perfect din of musketry in the woods. A large rebel battery on our left raked our troops with terrible effect, and soon our extreme left and then all the rest of our line gave way and came out of the woods in the greatest disorder, pursued by the enemy, who were yelling in their peculiar effeminate manner. They did not follow up their success by pushing round towards our right where Heintzelman was posted, but bore away towards the left sweeping round the south side of the field where McDowell was posted. Their progress was marked by their loud cheering.

From the time they began to advance until sundown, they never halted but swept everything before them like a hurricane. At sundown, they had swept away round to our rear and were within a short distance from the turnpike—our only line of retreat. Here they had met the veteran force of Sigel and Reno, who held them at bay until darkness put an end to the contest.

Our division relieved Sigel and confronted the enemy a few moments after sundown. The firing soon ceased. Skirmishers were thrown out on both sides and here we lay within hearing distance of each other until nine or ten o'clock that evening. A few shells were thrown on both sides when some officer, by giving orders in too loud a voice, indicated to the gunners the direction they were to aim. The last one thrown went through the top of a tree behind which I was lying, my company having deployed as skirmishers in front of our regiment. During this time, the army had retreated over Stone Bridge and up the hills towards Centreville. Towards midnight, we forded the stream and, our minds depressed with sorrow, bade a final adieu to the ill-fated fields of Bull Run.

General Pope is a most unblushing liar. In his official dispatch, he calls the result of the contest a victory when every man in the army knows that we were defeated at all points both Friday and Saturday and that too because at all points we were out-generaled. We lost the battle Friday because one brigade or division at a time was sent into the woods to be slaughtered. Had the great battle been fought Friday, we might have won, because the rebels received large reinforcements that night. Or had the battle been fought Sunday, we might have won, as Franklin's and Sumner's Corps would have been with us. Even on Saturday we might have won had not the flower of the army been cut up and disheartened the day before. Then the order of attack was faulty. Our lines should have been drawn perpendicular to those of the enemy instead of parallel. As it was, our great superiority in artillery was of no benefit to us as it was compelled for the most part to remain an idle spectator until our infantry had been defeated.

The battle was a great blunder. The defeat was as complete as that of the old Bull Run. The difference was that in this battle when a regiment was defeated it was not panic stricken, but rallied on its colors the moment it got behind the reserves. A rebel prisoner with whom I conversed told the truth when he said, "Boys, you can fight as well as we can, but Old Jackson is always one day ahead of you."

We have no general. Instead of continuing our retreat to Washington, General Pope halted at Centreville Sunday and Monday —long enough to allow the enemy to get in his rear and trouble his communications. The result was that we had to fight our way home, lose part of our train and execute a retreat in a hurry which we might have done at the proper time in good order.

In the battle of Monday afternoon, we were present at the firing of the first and last gun. At sun an hour high, the 6th New Hampshire was ordered forward. We found the field deserted by every regiment except the 50th Pennsylvania—and they were retiring in very bad order, but rallied and returned with us. Of the 2nd Brigade of our division, one regiment had got lost in the woods and one (the 21st Massachusetts) had lost all its field officers and a large proportion of its men by being decoyed by the rebels with an ambush.

From the time we entered the field until sundown, the 6th New Hampshire and 50th Pennsylvania were the only regiments under fire. I think it was Gen. Kearny who galloped up to us twice and said, "Hold out a little longer, boys, Kearny's Division is coming to relieve you." The rain fell in torrents and when we had fired away all our ammunition or our pieces had become so wet that they could not be discharged, we fixed bayonets to repel any attempt of the rebels to charge upon us. And we stood our ground until Kearny came up. . . .

Of all the brave boys who came out from New Hampshire with me, only nine followed me into Alexandria. The rest are all dead, sick, wounded or prisoners. And all to no purpose. Whatever may be our desires, I know that there are very few men in the army who have the least expectations of ever reducing the South. All who have been engaged in the events of the past two months know with what desperation the Southern troops fight and with what bad generalship our efforts are conducted, and have no hopes whatever of ever subduing them.

The Northern people get not the faintest idea from the newspapers of the true state of affairs at the seat of operations. The lying reports of our general and reporters beat anything that ever existed among the rebels. The whole army is disgusted. Are we disposed not to recognize impossibilities? We can do now voluntarily what we shall certainly be compelled to do when thousands of more lives have been sacrificed. You need not be surprised if success falls to the rebels with astonishing rapidity. They certainly have the force, the skill and genius to do it. . . .

At the great battle, we lay off our knapsacks when we went in and as we had no chance to get them after the battle, we have since had to lie on the bare ground with nothing but a thin flannel blouse to shield us from rain, dew and chilly night air. Last night when we reached our camp ground, there were only three company officers left. Several of the companies are commanded by sergeants, and companies A and D by corporals. I have not time to write more at present.

Yours Very Respectfully,

H. M. PEARSON

Henry Pearson was killed in action on May 26, 1864.

— ★ —

On August 19, 1862, Frederick Pettit* was mustered into the 100th Pennsylvania Volunteer Infantry as a corporal with Company C. These letters describe his first experience of combat at the Battle of South Mountain, Maryland.

Camp near Sharpsburg, Md.

Sept. 20th, 1862

DEAR PARENTS, BROTHERS AND SISTERS:

Having a little spare time this morning, I will commence to give you a short account of what our regiment has done since I came to it.

I overtook it about twenty miles from Washington at Brookeville, Md. It was dark when I found them. They had been resting a day to get provisions. The next morning, we started out a little before dark. Our rations are crackers, coffee, sugar, and beef when the cooks have time to boil it.

The next day, we started on our march again and passed through New Market, where the rebel pickets had been the night before. This town is eight miles from Frederick. After passing about two miles from the town, we halted and the cavalry and artillery were sent forward to reconnoiter. After waiting about

---

*Another letter by Frederick Pettit appears on page 201.

four hours, we again moved forward. About three miles from Frederick, we again halted.

The front skirmishers loaded their guns and advanced cautiously. The artillerymen ran two guns to the top of a hill on the right. But the rebels had gone. A shot or two at their rear sent them flying. We marched about a mile further and encamped two miles from the city. The next day we could plainly see the cannonading. We could not see any effects of it except a dead horse or two and houses turned into hospitals. After going some distance further, we encamped and lay down and slept during the remainder of the night.

The next morning we started early toward Middletown. It was not long before we heard cannonading in front. About a mile from Middletown, we found a large barn and bridge burned. But the stream was shallow, and we had no difficulty in crossing. After going a short distance further, we could see the batteries at work and hear the whizzing of the shells. The rebels occupied a wooded pass in the mountains. The turnpike runs through the middle of the pass. On the right of it, the rebels had a battery in a ploughed field and others on the left in the woods.

When we came in sight of the enemy, our division halted and our regiment was sent forward as skirmishers. We advanced along the turnpike in plain view of their batteries on the right until we came within a half mile of it. We halted and protected ourselves as well as we could under the bank at the side of the road. The enemy sent their shell amongst us thick and fast. They exploded above and all around us. Shortly an orderly came and told us to fall back. When we commenced to move, the shot and shell flew faster than ever. Our loss this time was only one man wounded, but if we had stayed fifteen minutes longer we would have been cut to pieces. . . .

We advanced up the hill steadily under a shower of shot until we came near the top of the hill, where the road ran between two high banks. Just had we halted when a number of cavalrymen and artilleries came rushing down upon us crying, "Clear the road for the cannon, we are beaten." Then the artillery came galloping down with the guns and caissons. And to make things worse, the rebels were sending grape shot and shell amongst us in a perfect shower.

We clambered out of the road as fast as we could, and our officers soon formed us in line of battle on the right of the road. We were ordered to fix bayonets and expected to make a charge, but after we started down the hill again and marched on up the valley about a mile, we halted, about faced, and started back across the hill. While coming up the valley, a number of men gave out; amongst them Lieutenant Morton. We saw him no more that day. We soon met General Wilcox and, as we were almost exhausted, he ordered us to lie down and rest.

After resting about three hours, we formed in line of battle. The rebels had advanced upon our cannon and we must drive them back. The 45th Reg. Pa. and 17th Michigan went in before us and drove them behind a stone wall. We then advanced to the top of the hill through a shower of musket balls. When we came to the edge of the woods, we halted and commenced firing. We were about as far from them as from our corn crib to the barn. They were in a lane behind a stone fence and we were in the edge of a woods with a clear lot between us. I fired eleven shots. Most of the boys fired fifteen before the rebels ran. The lane was piled full of killed and wounded rebels. . . .

I have a chance to send this now. We are all well and near the Potomac River. We move soon. I send you a rebel envelope I picked up on the battlefield.

F. PETTIT

Camp near Sharpsburg, Md.
Sept. 21st, 1862

DEAR PARENTS, BROTHERS AND SISTERS:

I have been so busy marching and fighting since I came to the regiment that I have not had time to write about anything else, but this pleasant afternoon I will write something about other things. As to playing soldier such as lying in camp drilling, etc., I know nothing about it. I never drilled a day in my life. All the soldiering

The 7th New York State Militia in camp

I have done is marching and fighting. Anybody can do this that is brave and strong enough.

I will commence with my equipments. My uniform is a pair of light blue pants and dark blue dress coat and cap. I have a haversack to carry grub, and a canteen to carry water. Every soldier must have these. Then I have a knapsack to carry clothes, blankets, etc. Besides these I carry a cartridge box with forty cartridges, a cap box full of caps and a bayonet in a scabbard, all on a belt round my waist supported by a strap over my left shoulder. I use a Springfield rifle, the best gun made. The cartridge box hangs on the right hip, the cap box in front, and bayonet on the left side. The haversack and canteen hang under the left arm. The knapsack is strapped upon the back. My gun I carry on my shoulder. I have a woolen blanket and a gum one. We have shelter tents. They are made of muslin and in two pieces each about two yards square. Each man carries a piece. Button the pieces together, stretch them on our guns, fasten them down with pegs and we have a house. Our knapsacks serve for pillows. When we don't march or fight, we write letters, read our bibles and cook and eat. We get along first rate.

> Your son and brother,
> F. PETTIT

— ★ —

John Burnham served as a lieutenant with the 16th Connecticut Volunteer Infantry. His letter is an account of the regiment's operations at the Battle of Antietam, Sharpsburg, Maryland, on September 17, 1862. With 26,193 casualties, it was the single bloodiest day of the Civil War.

———

> Mouth of Antietam Creek, Md.
> 4th October, 1862

MY DEAR MOTHER AND FAMILY,

I received a short note from Lottie enclosing extracts from newspapers about the fight of the 17th or the "Battle of Antietam."

LIEUTENANT JOHN BURNHAM

One thing is certain, it was a "big fight," as the sixteenth found to their severe cost, and although we got the best of it, on the whole I am unable to key myself up to a very high pitch of exultation over the day's work. We had the best of the fight because we had advanced our position during the day, but it was at heavy cost and the ground gained was contested inch by inch.

There has been no fighting since, and if our army was not pretty badly handled and about used up, I can imagine no earthly reason why we did not go at them the next day with a vengeance. We lay on our arms all day, the day after the battle, and all night the next night, expecting momentarily to be ordered forward, but we were not.

On Friday, we went on the field and gathered the dead and wounded. The rebels held the field in which the 16th were cut up so badly, and we had to leave the dead and wounded on that account over the whole of Thursday. They were there about forty-eight hours, but most of them, the wounded, said the rebs treated them kindly and gave them water. It was very hot weather, but fortunately there was a heavy rain on Thursday night and they managed to catch a canteen or two full of water by holding up the corners of their rubber blankets. One of our men, who was unable to get off the field, managed to pull off one of his boots and *caught water in that and drank it.*

I was on the field from noon until eleven o'clock at night of Friday, giving my personal supervision to the collection of the dead and wounded. You may be assured it was a trying position. To add to that, Col. Cheney and Maj. Washburne were both wounded, and Col. Beach took charge of the brigade and moved off with it, leaving me in charge of the regiment. I had the responsibility of the regiment on my shoulders for about twenty-four hours, and as everything was situated just then, it was quite long enough. Col. Beach and myself have neither of us been with the regiment since the third day after the battle, but we are only temporarily detached. He has just told me we are to go back to it tomorrow. If we are to go back at all, the sooner we do the better it will suit me, for we lose the run of things a little.

The position we occupy now is a pleasant one and I would like it if we could remain in it. Thus far, since we have been out, we have seen little but the "circumstance of glorious war," as someone has aptly said. Yesterday we saw a little of the "pomp" for the first time. The army was received by President Lincoln and Gen'l. McClellan, and of course we did our share. Our division happened to be the first one reviewed in Gen'l. Burnside's corps. As soon as the ceremony was over, the division and brigade commanders were ordered to dismiss their commands and join the President's escort.

If we had been in command of the regiment, we should have trotted back to camp, but I was lucky once again and as we stood for the time being in a Brig. Gen'l. and Adj. Gen'l.'s shoes, respectively, we had the honor of tagging old "Abe" around on his reviewing tour for a couple of hours and taking a look at between fifteen and twenty thousand men. I had seen "Abe" before but I thought him half so homely. He ought to be wise and good and honest.

Lottie wished me to write what were my personal feelings in the fight. I could sit down and talk to you and tell you all about it easily, but I find it more difficult to write how I felt. You have all heard a great deal about men going into battle and, after the fighting had commenced, forgetting all about what they were doing. This may be the case to some extent, but in my opinion nothing like what is represented. My position, when the regiment is making any maneuvers, is a very busy one, and when I was tearing about in that corn from one end of the line to the other carrying orders, I had no time to think of danger. But when, at one time as we were standing quietly, and all at once looking up the left I saw that rebel brigade which had outflanked us so prettily forming with the utmost order and coolness not much if any farther than halfway from our house to the Court House, and then, just as they were ready to come down on us, and before we had time to complete our change of front, I saw them haul up a battery in the same place and plant it, I am frank to confess that although I had no idea of running away I trembled.

You may call the feeling fear or anything you choose. I don't deny that I trembled and wished we were well out of it. I tried to do my duty and am satisfied. I came off the field side by side with Col. Beach. Afterwards we led the remnants of our own regiment and the 11th on to the field again through as hot a fire as I saw any time during the day. So far as my experience goes, I should not be sorry to see the war ended tomorrow without firing another shot, and yet I am a little eager to see one more battle. Not from any reckless desire for the excitement, but I have a little practical knowledge now and I think I should be more at home next time and perhaps do better. I should be considerable cooler, I have no doubt.

Lottie says Henry wished me to write particularly if it was true that the rebels deceived us with the "Stars and Stripes," and if they were dirty and ragged and lousy as they have been represented. I did not see their flag to notice particularly myself, but I can find fifty men and some officers in our regt. and in the 8th Conn. and 4th Rhode Island who would willingly take their oath that they carried our flag and shouted out to us not to fire on our own men. This cry "Don't fire on your own men" I heard distinctly in front of us myself and, supposing it to be from some regiment of ours who were in advance of us, I ordered the men near me to cease firing and they did so. We were in a field of thick heavy corn when you could not see twelve feet ahead and things were somewhat mixed at times. As I said, I cannot assert that I saw the rebels display our flag myself but so many of our men are so positive on that point that I have not the slightest doubt of it.

One thing, however, I did see, and that was the bodies of several dead rebels dressed in our blue uniforms, which they had taken in the recent fights near Manassas. That I saw myself, and one other thing I saw was this—one of our men by the name of Barnett had the picture of his wife and children hanging by a cord around his neck, and enclosed in a leather case. The rebs not only rifled his pockets but tore open this case and took the picture. The pockets of all our dead were emptied. In some instances, they cut the pockets out of the clothing, not stopping to examine them on the field. The shoes, too, were taken from all our dead bodies. This I think is a very plain indication of the state of the leather market in the Confederacy.

As to the second point, in relation to the condition of the rebels, I can answer that unequivocally I saw as many as five hundred prisoners I should think in one day and I never saw anything like it. Their hair was long and uncombed and their faces were thin and cadaverous as though they had been starved to death. It is of course possible that it is the natural look of the race, but it appeared mightily to me like the result of short fare. They were the dirtiest

In the trenches after the battle at Antietam, Maryland, July 1862

set I ever beheld. A regiment of New England paupers could not equal them for the filth, lice and rags.

One of our captains has a sweetheart in Frederick City. The father of the young lady was in our camp today to see the Capt., and he told me that when the rebels were in the city, some officers who had formerly known his daughter and his whole family, for that matter, called at his house, and it was actually the fact that after they had gone, they found lice crawling on their parlor furniture. This is a strong statement, but from the utterly wretched appearance of the large number I saw myself, I am not unprepared to believe it. Some gentlemen in Frederick told me that even the secessionists, although they did not and would not abandon their sympathy with the Confederacy, could not stand her soldiers and locked up their houses and lived on their Union friends to avoid them. . . .

Well, I have spun this out to an unusual length, and if you are interested or entertained enough when you get through to pay for the perusal, I shall be glad of it. If we move from here Monday, I will try and drop a line and let you know where we go, provided I know myself. I think we shall see more service yet before cold weather commences, and hope it may be to some purpose. If I am killed on the field I want my bones to lie in old Conn. by those of my father. . . .

To each and all of you, I can only repeat what I said to you the morning I left, which was that I hope to get through alive well and return to you in safety, but I prefer doing well even to that. I have been very careful, not only before but since I left home not to be at all boastful, and have studiously avoided making any rash statements of what I would do in this or that contingency. I had no idea how a fight would affect me. I have tried it now pretty thoroughly, and although I believe I "stood fire," I am no more inclined to brag than before.

I hope as I always have, that I may have the courage to do my duty well, not recklessly but with simple bravery and fidelity, so that if I fall you may have the consolation of knowing that I not only lose my life in a good cause but die like a man. One thing

I wish to say particularly—this romance about men being shot in the back is all a humbug. A mounted officer is as likely to be hit in the back, and more likely to be hit in the side, than in the front, and don't ever do an officer the injustice to think ill of him for such a wound. . . .

Bless you all.

Yours affectionately,
JOHN

— ★ —

The following letters were written by Samuel Edward Nichols, who served as a lieutenant with the 37th Massachusetts Volunteer Infantry.

———

Head Quarters 37th Regiment Mass. Vols.
Camp near Downsville, Md.
Oct. 17th, 1862

DEAR BROTHER FAYETTE,

Your letter sent with Phebe's was welcome, very so. Write often. Do not limit the number of your letters to that of mine. I am forced to plead a lack of stationery, and, what is more serious, a goneness of money. So do not mind if I do not respond as frequently as you write, and urge upon the folks the necessity of keeping me posted in all matters about home. All the matters, those even of minor importance; for everything about home multiplies in interest and in the same ratio as the distance from home and the time since separation have increased.

I am much pleased and interested in repairs going on at home. I always loved my home. "The Homestead on the Hillside" ever had attractions more powerful than any other spot on earth. Some of my fondest dreams have for their location the sloping fields and rude woodland of my father's farm. But place is not all that constitutes happiness. No; it is the hearts that cluster around that place. I feel that at all times and through every circum-

LIEUTENANT SAMUEL NICHOLS

stance, whether fortunate or adverse, the hearts which constitute our father's household in their beatings are ever true to those of their number who are so unfortunate as to be absent. I wish I could be with you at Thanksgiving time. But you must see that is denied me.

I give you the idea generally here among the soldiers, namely: that the war is hardly begun yet; that our three years will not see the war closed; that it is a war of extermination. But I believe differently. I may be over sanguine. I know I have seen no fighting service, but I think that does not interfere with my judgment; in fact, I believe those who have engaged in these hard-fought battles are unfit to form a correct opinion as to the durability of this rebellion.

It is like this: two armies are about to engage of nearly equal numbers. One side is termed the "South," the other the "North." They engage in a terrible conflict. It is doubtful what the result will be. Perhaps the "South," perhaps the "North," will be victorious; at any rate, the party that is victorious is almost as badly off as [the party that is] whipped. These men who engage liken the whole contest to this one struggle. They forget that the whole South almost exhausts her resources in getting up this one army and expedition, which is crippled by the almost crippling of one of our armies, while the North has exposed to loss only one of her armies. If the North should checkmate in every battle and each side destroy the other, in that event we should conquer; but you cannot, I cannot, no one can compute at what cost we gain our victory.

Ask father if he would not like to have a darky to work for him when I come home. I presume I might bring one home. Some of them are keen. It is sport to have them round.

The cannonading of yesterday was one continual roar from break of day to sunset. The air was all of a tremble, although the firing was twenty miles distant. I tell you it was exciting, even at this distance, to me. "But what must it be to be there?" I know it is awful, but at the same time it is so exciting as to make men forget themselves in the all glorious struggle.

I wish the thing were through with. You might think I should prefer to see one fight before coming home, but I think I could forego that if the thing could stop here. I have spilled my ink. I'll stop here. Write often. Be careful with your letters. Nothing like practice in these things.

Your affectionate Brother,
SAML. E. NICHOLS

————

Hd. Qrs. 37th Regiment Mass. Vols.
In camp at White Plains, Va.
7th Nov. 1862

MY DEAR FRIENDS AT HOME:

Received today your letter and I thought I would not write today, as I expected that we should be obliged to march before now; but we rest, strange to say, all day, and very likely we shall not have another such a halt for a number of days; so I thought I must write.

I received the money and thank you for it. We will be paid off sometime this month and I will then repay it. I am as anxious as you that you should go on with fixing up things about the house. Please do what you can in that line, for the old home on the hill is in my mind daily; and the thoughts which come to remembrance from the endearing experience of my entire life make endurable our long, tedious, and exhaustive marches.

Men with blistered feet, lame and swollen thighs, rheumatic shoulders and fevered body must put their thoughts most powerfully upon some cheering spot of their former life and march on mechanically. I do not say that I suffer much, because I have not as much as the men in ranks to carry; but I have intimate knowledge of persons, many of whose sufferings are correctly described by my language. What do you think of a man whose sufferings have gained so complete control over him and all sense of right which he formerly had (as he was a sober man), whose burning and exhausted body causes him to fall from the ranks, who in his despair shoots himself with his own musket? I know of such an instance.

Would you believe it, if I should tell you that I am brought in daily contact with a man in the prime of life, an honorable and thrifty mechanic from an enterprising town of western Mass., who has a small family at home that associates with highly respected families, whose sufferings here have become so unendurable that he meditates desertion and escape to Canada? There he can send for his family; and, almost a hermit, forever banished from friends who have known him from childhood, avoiding everyone who may have suspicions of the truth, he may live and die to shun the obloquy and disgrace this one act causes in the eyes of his country-men, especially in the eyes of those men at home who read every evening by the warm fire and over a fragrant cigar of our daring deeds and heroic suffering. Yet I say with all truthfulness that I know of such a man, that he comprehends all these consequences I have narrated, and not only these but also the fact of his liability to be shot in case of detection, that in the face of all these, which he spoke of today to me, he meditates desertion and such a disposition of himself as I have spoken of.

Now you say that somebody is awfully to blame; and still you are likely to blame men who cannot help it. The culprits who are woefully sinning should be punished; but may God direct the punishment, for man cannot properly. . . .

You think I am homesick. So I am. So I was before I enlisted. But, Mother, the same sense of duty which prompted me to enlist keeps me here and impels me to action. Were I home today under the same circumstances as on the 15th of last July, and had I had the experience I now have, my action would be the same. You cannot doubt me . . .

> Your
> SAMUEL

— ★ —

Constantine Hege* served as a private with the 48th North Carolina Volunteer Infantry. He wrote home after the First Battle of Fredericksburg, Virginia, on December 13, 1862.

Thursday morning
December 18, A.D. 1862
Near Fredericksburg, Va.

DEARLY BELOVED PARENTS:

I now once more have or take the opportunity of writing a few lines to you to let you know how affairs are here. I am somewhat unwell at present. I was taken with a chill and then a pain on my side night before last, but I now feel right better this morning. I think it was just a bad cold, which I had taken because I have nothing but old pieces of shoe on my feet. My toes are naked, and my clothing are getting ragged.

A Union cemetery near Hilton Head, South Carolina

*Another letter by Constantine Hege appears on page 71.

I have not got my box of clothing yet, and I don't know whether I ever will get them or not because the boxes are very often robbed at the depots. I wrote to you to bring me a box of clothing as soon as you possibly can, and come with them yourself so that you can be certain that I will get them because I need them very much.

There has been a very hard battle fought here at Fredericksburg Saturday. Our regiment was in the heart of the fight. I did not have to go into the battle because I am so near barefooted the colonel gave orders that all the barefooted men should stay at the camp. I can tell you I was glad then that my shoes did not come, because I would rather lose a hundred dollars than to go in a battle.

There was a great many killed and wounded, it is said that there were ten thousand Yankees killed during the battle. I do not know how many of our men were killed, but I know that there were a great many wounded. There were nineteen men wounded and one killed in our company. The human suffering, the loss of life and above all the loss of many a precious soul that is caused by war —would to God this war might end with the close of the year and we could all enjoy the blessing of a comfortable house and home one time more. I never knew how to value home until I came in the army.

It is thought that we would go on to Richmond in a few days. Tell Mr. Writes that I would be very glad to get a letter from him, tell Uncle Christos that I would like for some of them to write me, and I want you to write oftener and do not wait for me to answer every one of your letters before you write. I have not received any letter from you since Charles was out here. We have had very little chance to write out here because we have to drill twice a day in general and then have dress parade in the evening, and paper and ink is very scarce here, so I must close by giving you all the best wishes and respects and if we never meet on earth I hope to meet you in a better world.

> Your affectionate son,
> C. A. HEGE

— ★ —

After the First Battle of Fredericksburg on December 13, 1862, Hayward Morton,* a private serving in the 7th Massachusetts Volunteer Infantry, wrote home to give his account of the Federal defeat there, in which Yankee troops suffered 12,653 casualties.

———

Camp near Fredericksburg, Va.
Friday morning
Dec. 19th, 1862

DEAR MARTHA:

I received your very welcome letter Wednesday morning and before night I got three more letters, two from Francis and one from my old friend Tom Keith. Well, I will commence my adventures at three o'clock on Tuesday morning of the 11th day of Dec., at which time we busily engaged in packing up our bags preparatory to our advance on Fredericksburg.

As we have no great amount of furniture, we were soon on our way. We had to go for six or seven miles to march and we got there about nine o'clock A.M. I forgot to mention that as soon as it was light, we halted about an hour and a half and loaded our guns. On our way there we heard a heavy cannonading.

When we got in front of Fredericksburg, we found that our men were shelling the opposite side of the river so as to protect our men while they laid the pontoon bridges across the river. They got the one where we were to cross over done in the course of the afternoon but with one opposite Fredericksburg they did not have so good luck for the Rebel Sharpshooters picked off our men about as fast as they showed themselves, notwithstanding our forces were riddling the place with shell so that you would think that no one would care to stay in that vicinity.

The Irish Brigade were ordered to cross over in the pontoon boats and drive them from their hiding places. This they did, capturing about three hundred prisoners with the bridge unfin-

———

*Another letter by Hayward Morton appears on page 116.

ished. I have not heard what luck they had with it. We laid close by the banks of the river till sunset, when our brigade were to cross the river. The 2nd New Jersey Regiment went over first at a double quick and were deployed as skirmishers while the rest of the brigade filed to the right and left in line of battle, so as to support the pickets.

We remained here all night—one half the regt. resting at a time. We were not disturbed except by the cold frosty air. Friday morning, the troops commenced to cross the river by thousands, throwing out skirmishers and driving the enemy to his stronghold. We constituted the third line of battle all day Friday, Friday night and Saturday forenoon. Friday noon, the Rebs threw a few shells in our lines without doing much damage. Saturday morning, they commenced fighting quite lively. As the day advanced, the more the cannon roared and musketry rattled.

Saturday afternoon, about three o'clock, we were ordered to the extreme left to support our troops there. They had charged on the Rebs and had been repulsed and badly cut up. The ground was soft and muddy where we lay, and as there was plenty of cornstalks close by, we pickled into them so as to lay on them and just as we had got comfortably laid down, the infernal Rebs commenced shelling us with a vengeance. If we did not hug old mother earth, I am mistaken.

They kept shelling us till after dark. They had succeeded in killing and wounding a good many men, for they had complete range of us. About nine o'clock, we were ordered back to the rear. We were not sorry to leave that part of the field. We did not have but two men wounded while some regiments had all the way from ten to thirty killed and wounded. Sunday, we drew rations. This day was very quiet and there was not much firing.

Monday morning, before light, we were ordered to the front. We expected to have to take it before night, but were happily disappointed. The Rebs were bringing up some guns to shell us when our guns opened on them and they skedaddled. Towards midnight on Monday night, we unexpectedly received orders to fall back to the rear. I soon saw that our whole army was in motion. I came to the conclusion that they had made a bad job of it and were on the skedaddle for the opposite side of the Rappahannock and I soon found that to be the true reason, for the Rebs held one of the strongest positions, and they appear to mean to hold it.

We covered the retreat. Our brigade was the last one to cross over back again. So we were the first to cross and the last to come back. We fell back about a mile from the river and halted. We had no sooner got off our equipments than it began to rain quite hard. As it was near daylight, I pulled my rubber blanket over my head and was soon in the land of dreams.

When I woke up, it had stopped raining and was clearing off cold. I got me some breakfast and coffee, and as soon as it began to dry up, Mason and I began to rig up our tent. We stayed in this place Tuesday and Wednesday. Wednesday forenoon, I went out on to the hill to see the Rebs, for we can see all the ground we have occupied on the opposite side of the river. I could see the Rebs' line of battle, also their pickets and men looking over the field to see what they could pick up. Thursday morning, we moved again two or three miles to a fine woods as I ever saw. Our Col. told us we should probably stop here two or three weeks.

You wanted to know if we had any snow here and if it was as cold as it is at home at this time of the year. We had a snow storm here about two weeks ago and it stayed as much as a week. I don't think it is quite so cold here as at home, although it has been pretty cold here sometimes.

I see you are having a good time at home going to the singing parties. I should write more letters to the boys if I had time and could get stamps. The story about having nothing but hard bread and raw pork to eat is a hoax, for we had a chance to cook our meals every day when we crossed the river. On Tuesday eve, some of our men went a skirmishing in the rear, and as there was a large plantation near by, the boys found plenty of pigs and poultry and flour and meal and most everything you can think of that's eatable.

The day that we crossed over, a Rebel rode up on horseback close by where our men were throwing over the pontoon bridges and cheered Jeff Davis, but his noise was soon stopped by one of our men shooting him through the body. I saw him when I crossed over, and he was a fine looking young man as you very often see.

When I was down on the left on Saturday, they were carrying off men who had lost their legs, arms and had been otherwise wounded. I did not hear a groan from one of them, although some of them must have been in great pain.

We took several prisoners. It was quite interesting to talk with them. Someone asked one of them how far it was to Richmond. He said we should have to go over two hills, then get over a Stonewall, go through a Longstreet and by that time we should end up on a Lee shore. Pretty good, that.

I have written so much today I am getting tired, so I will bring my letter to a close. Hope this will find you smart as a cricket, with love six feet long and twenty feet circumstance. Give my best respects to all enquiring friends, and my love to all the family.

From Your Affectionate Brother,
MORTON

— ★ —

Horatio Newhall served as sergeant with Company C, 44th Massachusetts Volunteer Infantry. Sergeant Newhall's letter is an account of his regiment's activities along the coast of North Carolina from December 11–22, 1862.

December 22nd, 1862

DEAR MOTHER:

I am happy to be able to write you of my safe return from our second expedition, for which I hope I am duly thankful. I have returned safe and sound without scratch or scar and without any disease with the exception of a cold in the head caused by a too great exposure of my nose on frosty nights.

We have been on a very successful expedition since I wrote last,

SERGEANT HORATIO NEWHALL

have been gone ten days, travelled 160 miles for three battles and lived the whole time on hard tack and coffee and three days' rations of salt horse. This is an outline of what has happened in the last fortnight and I shall try to give you some account of our trip, telling you this at first to set your mind at rest.

I am so confused in my mind since my return that I can hardly collect my ideas into any kind of shape. Why it is I do not know unless it is during my trip my mind and body were at a greater strain than ever before *in my life* and the relaxation has been so great that I feel like sitting perfectly still or sleeping all the time. Perhaps you may understand what I mean by this feeling.

Since my return, I have received ten letters from home, one of them from Claflin, one from Sarah Field, and I believe the balance from you and George. They contain so much that I shall not attempt to answer them today at all except to tell you that the money and rhubarb came to hand safely and that I have heard nothing from my Christmas box as yet. The pickles and bundle in Sam's box I got on my return safely and they have done me much good already. I shall commence another letter when this is finished and will try to answer yours at that time. I wrote George a note the 10th telling him we were to start the next day. Did you receive it?

We started on the morning of the 11th at six o'clock with a force of fifteen thousand men and fifty-six pieces of artillery and where we were going was a secret known only to our leaders. I have never seen so large a force of men together. It was a grand sight to see them file by us and string out along the road as we formed in columns just outside of Fort Potter. I do not know how long a line we made but as far as the eye could reach was nothing but infantry, artillery, baggage wagons, ambulances and cavalry, (of the latter we had 1500). We carried more on our backs this time than before, for we had our knapsacks and woolen blankets so that we had quite a load on our backs.

The first day we made twelve miles and at night we camped all together in an immense field. I shall never forget the sight we saw as we marched into the field at ten o'clock P.M. As far as the eye could reach on all sides were campfires, making it appear that the whole surface of the earth was on fire and the heavens were as red as blood with the reflection. On the borders of the camp were woods and the men had set fire to the pitch pine trees, so that the woods were in a blaze also. It was a wild sight, and one I never expect to see again. I have seen the camps and wood on fire a great many times but I never saw anything as grand before or since.

We were pretty tired for our knapsacks worried our backs badly, but the men went right to work and brought in fence rails and it was not fifteen minutes after we marched in before every man had his cup of coffee steaming on the fire and was munching his hard tack. We had had no dinner and were hungry. Then all turned in, for the night, that is, we spread out rubber blankets and rolled ourselves in the woolen ones and then laid down with our feet to the fire. We slept soundly all night.

The next day we started before daybreak and marched all day without a halt, making eighteen miles, and went into camp at ten P.M. I was very tired this night, but a good cup of coffee and hard

The long line of tents at Morris Island, South Carolina

tack and a night's rest revived me. At this point was a long swamp
with water the whole length. The rebels had felled large trees for
a mile across the road so that our pioneers had to work all night
to clear the road that we might pass the next day.

We started the next morning at sunrise and marched through
their swamp to our knees in water the whole way. The trees they
cut were not more than two rods apart. Some of them would
measure three feet in diameter, they were all those large straight
pitch pines. This day the advance had skirmishing the whole way
out. We only made seven miles. We took several prisoners and in
one place I saw seven dead rebels lying on the side of the road.
They were killed by our cavalry.

At night, the advance came upon the enemy formed in line of
battle five miles this side of Kinston but not in large force and we
drove them, taking two pieces of artillery from them. General
Wessells' (formerly Casey's) brigade was in advance and we saw
nothing of it, but we camped on the field and went to bed with
the prospect of a fight the next day at Kinston.

The next morning we heard the enemy were in a strong position before Kinston. Soon after daybreak, we heard the cannon
and were pushed forward almost at double quick. We were the
third brigade and where we came up all the others were already
engaged. The enemy were formed behind a large swamp and the
only road through it was guarded by the cannons. . . .

When we came up to the swamp, we were formed in line of
battle and laid down on the ground to keep away from the bullets,
which were being thrown around rather carelessly by the rebels.
The 10th Connecticut Regiment marched in front of us and went
right into the fight before us. Soon the orders came for our regiment to advance through the swamp and support the 10th Connecticut. We advanced through it, the cannonball, shell and bullets
cutting the trees over our heads. One of our men, Sergeant Howe,
Company H, was wounded in the head. The black swamp mud
was up to our waist and briars and grapevines grew wild, making
it almost impossible to go ahead at all. We managed to push
through it however and reach the other side about one-eighth of

a mile. All through the swamp were men lying dead and wounded in the mud by dozens. . . .

I had never seen a real battlefield before and it sickened me to see such a sight. Some dying, some dead and others going to the rear without help but bleeding badly. Rebels and union men lying together, large trees cut in two, broken muskets and horses lying in all directions, all kinds of equipment and swords and bayonets, giving me for the first time an idea of what a battlefield was. We lost in this battle about 250 killed and wounded. The rebels must have lost more, for our artillery played upon them as they retreated across the bridge with good effect.

I would have liked to have brought home some trophies from the field and could have sent home some splendid rebel rifles and many other things which were lying about, but it was impossible to carry away anything, for we were already overloaded for such rapid marching. The 10th Connecticut Regiment was badly cut up. It went into the fight with 317 men and lost 106 in killed and wounded. We should have shared the same fate had we gone in at the same time.

I never saw such a mean looking set as the prisoners were. They had all kinds of uniforms. Mostly their uniforms were of a dirty gray homespun. They seemed rather to like the idea of being prisoners, and we fed them with hard tack from our haversacks, for they looked and were half starved, our men having succeeded in putting out the fire on the bridge we marched across and took possession of the town. They allowed us to spend the night here and we were glad enough to do so. We were very tired. We found plenty of lumber here and made beds and fires of it and had the best night's rest of any during the march. We did not occupy houses as guards were put in there to protect them. The town is small like all and every town and city here. The rebels burned all the cotton and every street had one or two large bonfires made of it.

The next day (the 15th), we recrossed and burned the bridge and marched sixteen miles toward Whitehall and camped for the night about four miles from the town. The morning of the 16th, we broke camp at sunrise and soon began to hear firing in the advance.

We were second brigade in line. Where we came up, we found the rebels had burned the bridge and were disputing our passage of the river. The river here is quite narrow and the woods thick on the opposite side and a narrow belt of woods on our side, behind that cornfields. Our *object* was as far as I could see not to pass the river but engage the rebels and keep them where they were while our main force went on by a road near the river and gained a march on them towards Goldsboro.

Where we came up, we were ordered to file through the field and form the bank of the river behind a rail fence. We pushed forward and gained our place but not without loss, for the *enemy* saw us and they directed their fire at us. The first cannon ball that came killed two men in Company A, blowing off their heads, but our men marched over their bodies without hesitation and gained our place without further loss. I believe we were ordered to lie down and load and rise and fire when we saw anyone to fire at. Occasionally we gave them a full volley by way of variety.

All the men were strangely cool in this, our first fight. I felt as cool as if I were firing at a target and when a man was knocked over and taken to the rear it did not affect me in the least. Why it was so I cannot tell, for I must say that before we went into it, I could not help feeling a little afraid of those bullets. But when once I had discharged my rifle, I did not mind the bullets buzzing around my ears in the least. I did once try to dodge them and was angry at being obliged to lie down to load. All our men felt the same I afterward found. We fought here two hours and lost nine of our regiment killed and fourteen wounded, a very small number considering the heavy fire of the enemy. Only the right wing of our regiment was engaged, the left being out of range. Our company had three wounded, one of them but slightly. . . .

After two hours, we found that the sharpshooters of the enemy were in trees on the opposite side where our rifles could not touch them. The colonel therefore sent for Belger's battery to come and help. We told them where to aim. The first gun they fired cut a tree in two, and down came three of the rascals. Orders now came to us to form in [the] rear of Belger's battery and support it and we lay for another hour on the ground, the bullets often passing within six inches of our backs. I expected every minute to feel one rasp down my back. This was the most trying part of the fight for us, for we could not fire a gun in return, only lie there to protect the battery. The orders now came to leave and join the main force on the road and the fight was over. The whole loss on our side in this fight was two hundred killed and wounded.

Our last fight was seventeen miles further on at Evertsville, where we were to destroy the railroad and railroad bridge of Wilmington and Goldsboro Roads. And this I afterward learned was the *whole object of our expedition*. We were not in this fight, as it was mainly fought with artillery. Our batteries did terrible execution—Belger's battery in particular did nobly. The rebels made three charges from the woods to take Belger's battery, but he waited every time until they got within half musket shot and then gave them a volley of grape and canister and mowed them down *by hundreds*.

All this time, our infantry was at work tearing up the track and then in burning a long bridge. When the flames of the bridge and smoke appeared, General Stevenson rode down the line saying, "Go home boys, the object of our expedition is accomplished." And cheer upon cheer told how willing the men were to turn for home.

We could have taken Goldsboro at this time, for we were only three miles from the city, but it would have taken a large force to hold it and we were almost entirely out of provisions and ammunition. So we took road for home that night. The next day we made Kinston, and having taken our wounded who had been left here into ambulances, started the next morning for New Bern. They told us that by taking a mirror road we could get to New Bern that night, travelling twenty-five miles. The men braced themselves for it, determined to go through though they were very footsore, but after we had gone fifteen miles, we found this road impassable. So we were obliged to take another. Still, General Stevenson wanted to get our brigade through that night (a distance of thirty-two miles) and as we pushed along without halting, every now and then men would drop out, unable to go further, and when we were within eight miles of New Bern the word came that anyone who chose to could drop out and come in at their leisure. So I made up my mind to drop out and I left the ranks for the first time in the march.

I was very tired, having travelled twenty-four miles that day, and thought I should feel better to rest awhile and then go on. A number of my friends were cooking coffee in the woods here. I joined them and put on my pot to boil. Our number soon increased to about twenty-five, and after a sumptuous meal of coffee and hard tack, we came to the conclusion to spend the night where we were and come in the next morning. So we detailed a watch to keep the fire going and all turned in and slept soundly all night, rose before daybreak and got into New Bern in time for a late breakfast.

This was the night which George mentioned in his letter of the 20th as being so cold. He said he thought of me that night. I was pretty cold but we had a good fire and did not mind it. Every night during our march the ground froze hard and we did not sleep under cover once. I cannot spend any more time describing this expedition and have only told you the facts right through without trying to embellish them. I could only say that this march was the hardest piece of work I *ever* did in my life and I am thankful I came through it so well. I'm as well as ever now and could go through the same tomorrow as well as before. My feet held out favorably and my shoes are still good.

I think the 44th can now claim to have seen service and I'm sure we all feel like veterans. Hope we shall not be sent off any more at present for I think we worked pretty hard so far and deserve a little rest. These marches are the severest kind of service and I'm surprised to find how much fatigue and exposure men can bear. . . .

Give my love to father and George, to the Mays and Kimballs, to Martha and Anna Richardson and all my friends, and keep your spirits up until next summer when I hope we shall meet again.

Your affectionate son,
HORATIO

— ★ —

Hayward Morton* served as private with the 7th Massachusetts Volunteer Infantry.

———

Camp near Fredericksburg, Va.
Tuesday morning, Dec. 23rd, 1862

DEAR BROTHER:

I received your very welcome letters a few days ago and was very happy to hear from you as well as sorry to learn that you have been so unwell lately.

We were detailed to go out on picket yesterday morning. The rest of our company being reserves and I having nothing to do but lay around on the ground, I thought that I would while away a few moments by addressing you a few lines. It has been very cold here for a week past, but yesterday the weather began to moderate

Members of the 114th Pennsylvania Infantry playing cards

*Another letter by Hayward Morton appears on page 104.

and this morning the sun shines out bright and warm as in the summer time.

Our pickets are posted all along the banks of the Rappahan-nock, and the regiment's pickets are also posted on the opposite side in plain sight. The pickets do not fire at each other now as they used to on the Peninsula, so that there is no more danger in being out on picket now than there is in laying around in camp. We and the reserves lay a little ways back from the pickets in a ravine close by an old grist mill. We have to stay out on picket three days.

The men are sick of the war and are deserting from this regi-ment. The soldiers are down on the Abolitionists and say they will give them particular fits when they get home again. There is no love of your nigger men here in the army among the pri-vates. We all hate the sight of a nigger worse than a snake, and when we are on a march and come across any of them, they call them all manner of names, throw stones and sticks at them. In fact, anything is not too bad for one of them damn niggers as the boys call them. . . .

What do the people say at home about the fight at Fredericks-burg? Do they think any more of Burnside than they do of McClellan now that he has been defeated? I have yet seen no account of the Battle of Fredericksburg, no newspapers having been brought into camp yet.

There is some queer nuts here in our regiment. I never laughed so much in my life as I have since I joined the regiment. One of the boys wanted to know how many horse power the engine was where his chum worked before he enlisted. He got for an answer four Ram cats. And that's the way they keep it a going all the time. I shall never be sorry that I enlisted if I get out of the scrape right side up with care. . . .

From Your Brother,
MORTON

— ★ —

William R. M. Slaughter served as a second lieutenant with Company L, 6th Alabama Volunteer Infantry. His letter is an account of the regiment's activities at the First Battle of Fredericksburg on December 13, 1862.

———

Camp near Grace Church, Va.
Jan. 4th, 1863

MY DEAR SISTER,

Your kind and interesting letters of the 8th and 13th were both received through the obliging mails of "Cousin Sally" in due season; and owing to circumstances, over which I had no control, the dawn of a new year finds them still unanswered. . . .

Your last was written upon the 13th of December, and upon that day the great battle of Fredericksburg was fought. Had you known the dangers to which I was exposed so constantly upon that bloody day, at the time of writing that letter, would not your hand have trembled?

But since you write that my descriptions of the battles are interesting to you, I will give you a detailed account of the transactions of the two or three days prior and subsequent to the fight.

Daniel H. Hill's division, which constituted the extreme right wing of our army, was quietly encamped four miles from Port Royal, one of the oldest villages in Va., and twenty miles below Fredericksburg. The extreme left wing of our army rested upon the Rappahannock River, above Fredericksburg. Burnside had determined to cross the river at Port Royal, as soon as his pontoon train should have come up from Aquia Creek.

As soon, however, as Jackson's corps arrived, it was posted in the vicinity of Port Royal and constituted a force rather larger than Burnside wished to compete in the passage of the river, where the natural advantage of the positions of the two armies were more nearly equal than they were at Fredericksburg. So when Burnside's train of bridges did arrive, he resolved upon a different course. His plan then was by a sudden passage of the river and a vigorous assault upon Longstreet's right wing to separate the two corps of our grand army and whip them in detail. A million of men could not have prevented his passage of the river at Fredericksburg; for holding a range of hills, upon which was mounted his heavy siege guns, so he swept for three miles the perfectly level and highly cultivated plains upon the side of the river.

The policy for us to pursue was to detain him in his passage of the river until Jackson's corps could arrive at the scene of action, then to withdraw and permit him to throw his forces across, but to keep him pinned to the river bank. About daybreak, on Thursday morning, Dec. 11th, the enemy commenced the bombardment of Fredericksburg. About sunrise, their gunboats at Port Royal turned loose upon our batteries. The firing below soon ceased, for the gunboats dropped down river, while that above became incessant, and continued so throughout the day.

That night, the enemy threw a pontoon bridge across the river, and sent forces enough over to occupy and hold the town. The next day the cannonade was resumed and continued with unabated fury throughout the day. In the meantime an alarm was given at Port Royal, and Rodes' Brigade was sent down to the river to relieve our pickets; but the alarm proving false, we returned to camp and stayed there the remainder of the day.

About sunset, orders came for us to report immediately to Fredericksburg. That night we marched eighteen miles and camped within one mile of our position in line of battle. It was now three o'clock A.M. and we laid ourselves down to sleep and rest. The Yankees had thrown across their sixth pontoon bridge the day before, and their entire army was now effecting its passage.

At early dawn, we were aroused from our slumbers and marched into position. Our forces, in three lines of battle, occupied a series of slight elevations, which described the circumference of a large semicircle, the concave surface being turned toward the enemy. Our forces extended from the left point of the semicircle nearly to the center and our faces were turned down the river.

Our front line was protected by [a] railroad embankment upon our left. The morning was foggy, but the plain lay stretched out in quiet beauty before us.

About nine o'clock, the dark masses of the enemy, in four lines of battle, moved forward in splendid order to the attack. The artillery of both armies now commenced, and, as we were lying immediately in rear of and in line with one of our batteries, we suffered occasionally the loss of some poor fellow from the enemy's random shots. Our division constituted the right wing of our line, so we could see but little of what was going on in front. Soon, however, we heard the rattle of small arms, and we knew that our infantry was engaging the enemy.

The enemy now made a demonstration to turn our right flank. Gen. Lee dispatched three couriers simultaneously to Gen. Hill with orders for him. He dispatched his most reliable brigade immediately to the front to prevent this movement of the enemy. In files of four, our brigade moved off to the front at right angles with our line of battle and opposite our extreme right wing. The enemy's infantry, fearing that we might turn their left flank by outflanking them, retired, but their artillery turned loose a perfect storm of shell and solid shot upon our advancing columns with the view of breaking our line.

One solid shot (it makes my hair stand on end to think of it) passed between two files of our company and could not have missed me by more than six inches. I know this, for I saw the ball. It passed about six inches in front of my thighs. I think it was fired from a six pounder rifle gun.

As the enemy retired, we again returned to our original position. While we were returning, our whole line charged the enemy with one loud yell. They were reeling, staggering, breaking, as they fled precipitately from the field. His second line of battle, however, maintained its position, and the two armies stood confronting each other still. Quiet reigned everywhere over the whole field, with the exception of an occasional exchange shot from the artillery.

Don't misunderstand me to say that the enemy's second line

maintained our attack. Our forces did not advance far enough to attack it, for it was supported by too many powerful batteries of artillery. There was in our immediate front the famous Lexington Battery, consisting of eighteen twenty-four pounder rifle guns. There was, however, an order for our whole line to move forward at dusk and charge this line of batteries, but the order was countermanded. Our brigade did not receive the countermanding order and continued to advance. On account of the density of the woods, the sixth and twenty-sixth Alabama Regiments became separated from the remainder of the brigade. Gen. Rodes soon halted his brigade, but the two left regiments kept a ripping. . . .

The next day was a continued picket fight, with an occasional artillery shot, we supporting the second line of battle. Monday it was our turn to take position in the front line, which we did about daybreak. The Yankee's line was about six hundred yards from ours, in full view, and our pickets were about 200 yards apart.

Soon after light, they appeared with a flag of truce to collect their wounded between the picket lines, which was granted. The pickets now laid down their guns, and, meeting upon halfway ground, such another swapping of buttons, knives, pipes and giving salt and coffee for tobacco you never heard of. The wounded upon both sides were collected. Poor fellows! How pitifully they groaned; they had lain upon the field from Saturday to Monday without food or water. Another flag was brought out soon after noon, for the burial of the dead. It was granted and the dead were carried out to a midway point and exchanged.

About night, we were ordered to tear up the railroad track and lay it in piles for the purpose, it was said, for protecting us from artillery. As day started, it commenced to drizzle rain. When light came, not a "Yank" was to be seen. Our skirmishers pursued, capturing many stragglers.

It was then that a most melancholy accident happened. I. M. Iverson from Lowndes Co., and of the Third Ala. Reg., was among the skirmishers, but Iverson advancing found a splendid Yankee overcoat, which he put on. He was a very brave boy and as the line continued to advance, he got some distance ahead. One of the Southern Rifle Company, seeing him advance, and mistaking him for a Yankee, shot him, the ball penetrating his heart and killing him instantly. . . .

I walked over to where the Yankee lines of battle had been. There lay their dead in great heaps unburied. They had been stripped of all their outer garments, and especially of their shoes, by our men. The grass upon that portion of the field where many of them had fallen had been set on fire by the explosion of shells. Their hair, whiskers, eyebrows and lashes had been burned, and their faces and hands had been partially roasted.

I noticed that the bodies of the dead Yankees upon the plains of Fredericksburg were of tall and slender men. Heretofore they have hurled their foreign population into places of danger, but we have for the most part killed them out, and from this time on, I think, we will play havoc with the real genuine blue-bellied Yankees themselves.

There will be more fighting here this winter, I think. Some of our troops are building winter quarters, and it is reported that the Yankees are doing the same thing upon the other side of the river. Many of our troops will be sent down to protect the Southern coast and especially the North Carolina coast. It is surmised here that Hill's Division will be sent off. We hope not, for we are not anxious to fight both winter and summer. . . .

Sister, I know "brevity is the soul of wit" and I believe that if my letters were shorter, they would not be so boring to you to read. I dislike to start out with a description and not give it in full, but I tell you it often puts patience to the bitter test. You no doubt see a great difference both in the composition and penmanship between the beginning and end of each of my letters. I will not annoy you with any more such long letters, but will try to be shorter and sweeter. . . .

Your affectionate brother,
RHADDIE

— ★ —

Edward Wood served as a private with the Chicago Board of Trade Battery. His letter was written after the Union victory at the Battle of Stones River (Murfreesboro), Tennessee, which lasted from December 31, 1862, to January 2, 1863.

———

January 12, 1863

DEAR BROTHER WILL,

You will think when you have read this that I have become an inveterate grumbler, but all our former experience, when compared with what we have undergone since leaving Nashville, seems but a pleasure excursion. I had no idea what powers of endurance man possessed until I saw them tested as I think I now have, to the uttermost. 'Tis beyond my power to give you anything like a faithful description of the scene, but [I] will only relate a few of the incidents that came directly under my observation.

We left Nashville the Friday morning after Christmas and traveled all day in a pelting rain, and stopped for the night in an old cotton field which the rain and the tramping of thousands of men and mules and wagons had converted into a vast sea of ankle-deep mud. Arriving at this delectable spot about 9 P.M. dark as Egypt, we tied our horses to the wheels of the gun and then essayed to make a pot of coffee, which we finally accomplished using water from a convenient mudhole; but "that's the way we have it in the army." After supper we did not sing a hymn but made use of some expletives which you doubtless consider contraband and retired for the night, made a bed by cutting a cedar tree and crawling into the branches and let it rain.

Next morn, we hitched up before daylight, but did not move from our positions as there was a strong force of rebs ahead of us with which our advance guard was fighting all day. We were obliged to stand by our horses all day, as the roar of cannon and muskets was very distinct and made them very restive. It rained in torrents all day and we had a lovely time, I assure you.

Just at night, we pitched tents and, putting in evergreens to keep us out of the mud, passed what we call a comfortable night. Sunday was a bright warm day, and we spent the time in clearing the mud from our horses and harness until two o'clock, when we were ordered to advance. We camped that night near a small town called La Vergne.

Next day we moved forward a few miles to Stewart's Creek, where we were ordered to halt and protect the pioneers while building a bridge. Meanwhile, the rest of the army moved on towards Murfreesboro. The bridge was completed about three o'clock in the morning. Then we moved forward and came up with the army in line of battle about ten o'clock.

We were not engaged that day and at night were sent to the left to hold a ford of Stones River, where the enemy was expected to cross. We worked late that night felling trees and building breastworks, and soon after we laid down it commenced to rain. There was no attack that night. Early Wednesday morn the rebs made a furious attack on our center, driving our troops in all directions. We were ordered to the front and took our position near the "pike" and opened on the rebs with canister; soon driving them back, our troops rallied and, following them, again regained the ground lost in the morning. We advanced about a quarter of a mile and took a position on a ridge, which we held all day.

Now the work commenced in earnest. The rebs formed in the woods in front of us, and three times during the day charged on us, we pouring in all the time a continuous shower of shell and canister. At one time they got within 200 feet of us when the pioneers who were supporting us sprang to their feet and poured in a volley of musketry which was too much for them. They broke and ran. All this time, they had four batteries playing on us from the woods, pouring into our very midst a perfect shower of shot and shell from which we suffered very severely.

One solid shot struck Finney and Wiley, cutting them nearly in two. And soon after, a shell struck Stagg and, bursting just as it struck, tore him all to pieces, but not a man wavered. We now turned our attention to these batteries, and soon silenced one and compelled the others to retire.

During the engagement, Gen. Rosecrans rode up and said if we could hold our position for one hour, the day was ours, but if we gave way the whole right wing of the army was lost. Stokes [battery commander] replied that he would hold it as long as there was a button on our "coats." . . .

After the moon was up, we buried the dead, and sent our caissons for ammunition, as we were nearly out, having fired about 1200 rounds that day. During the night, we watered our horses and fed them and made a little coffee in a cup, not being allowed to have much fire, and prepared for warm work next day.

It commenced early in the morn. The rebs crawled close up to us under cover of a fog, but we were on the look out and grape and canister soon did the business for them. Thursday we had no very heavy work, the fighting being more to the right, but the sharpshooters kept up a continuous rattle all day. About three o'clock in the afternoon, Sexton and I lay down on a rock to rest and fell asleep, when a bullet passed just over our faces and woke us up, and we kept awake "I bet you."

Two or three of the prisoners, who were now our warm friends, crawled down through the bushes and found the rascal who shot at us up in a tree. They drew a bead on him, and he tumbled instantly.

About ten o'clock Thursday night, we were relieved and sent to the rear, where we had supper—the first meal we had eaten since Wednesday morn. Friday morn we advanced again, when the rebs poured into us a heavy fire from two batteries. Their guns were loaded with brass balls and railroad iron. Three of our batteries soon silenced them, when we were again sent to the rear. About three o'clock, we had a good dinner, considering the circumstances. It was rather trying to a man's nerves to eat in such a place, for now and then a shell would drop in our immediate vicinity. For half an hour an ominous silence pervaded the whole line, when on the left wing was heard the most deafening roar of musketry, and about fifty pieces of artillery opening at the same time rendered the scene indescribably awful. We were ordered forward.

On reaching a little ridge, the whole scene was before us. For about half an hour, the conflict raged with a fury unparalleled. Then our troops began to give way, and it looked dark, I tell you. The rebs sent up a cheer that rent the heavens, and we started a cheer that was taken up by our lines, and the 19th coming up started in with their "Tiger" cheer, and our forces rallied and started for a charge.

We were now passed by guns and caissons in full retreat who said to us: "Don't go ahead, you will be captured." But just at this time Negly [battery commander] rode up and said, "For God's sake, Captain, if you can do anything, do it or we are lost." He made no reply, but gave the order forward. We started with a yell, our troops cheering and following on the run. We advanced beyond our lines and unlimbered on a ridge and directly opposite us on a high bank. On the other side of the river was a whole battery, and as it was now dark we could see every flash of their guns directly on our eyes. The infantry passed us down into a valley, driving back rebs at the point of the bayonet, we at the same time engaging the reb battery, which we silenced, and our forces dashing through the river and up the opposite bank took five of their pieces. We crossed the river and in a few minutes occupied the very ground on which the reb battery had stood. The ground was so thickly strewn with dead and wounded that it was only with great care that we could drive without running over them. . . .

We had no more fighting after this, but late Saturday night there was a heavy fight on our right. During Saturday night, the rebs evacuated, and Sunday we moved to the woods where we had first encamped and built our breastworks, which we called "Fort Stone," where we remained till Tuesday, when we moved into Murfreesboro. We are now encamped on ground lately occupied by the rebs. There the pioneers are building another bridge and a stockade for its defense. Weather warm and pleasant and we have dry clothes and something to eat and tents. . . .

We passed the time from Wednesday morn till Saturday night with only three meals and drenched nearly all the time, but few of the boys are sick. I wonder there is one of us alive. Provisions were very scarce. The wagons were compelled to run to Nashville on Wednesday and many were captured and burnt. Ours all escaped. Gen. Rosecrans in his telegram to Gen. Halleck said that we saved the day and so we did. Nothing but our charge on Friday ever rallied the troops and drove the rebs from our left.

We suffered more for tobacco than food during those exciting days. Our source of supply was from the rebs, and we searched dead men's pockets for the precious weed with an avidity which gold could not have excited. This may seem shocking to you, so it does to me now, but we thought nothing of it then. Think of the contrast between your happy New Year and ours.

I was sitting on my horse when a bullet passed through my coat and struck that big knife you gave me and glanced off. I said to the driver behind me, "It is too hot for us here," and dismounted. I had scarcely reached the ground when a spent ball struck my shoulder, doing no damage beyond a slight bruise. I thought it rather hot here, and began to think of mounting again, when a solid shot struck near the gun and bounded just over my horses. I concluded that if I stayed on the ground, I should not have so far to fall, and so remained on terra firma the rest of the day.

ED

— ★ —

James Coburn* served as a corporal with the 141st Pennsylvania Volunteer Infantry.

Camp Pitcher
January 18th, 1863

DEAR FOLKS AT HOME:

Today I witnessed what I never did before, the drumming out of a deserter. He belonged to the 63rd P.V. (of our brigade),

---

*Another letter by James Coburn appears on page 234.

deserted last July, was caught some four months after, and had just had his trial before a court martial—found guilty and sentenced to forfeit all that was owing to him, have his head shaved, be branded with D on the right hip in the presence of the whole brigade and be drummed out.

We were under orders to march today at one o'clock P.M., but owing to the cold weather (or something else), it was postponed for twenty-four hours, and so today at two o'clock the regiments formed to witness the dishonorable discharge of said deserter. The prisoner was called out, his head shaven, the iron heated, pants turned down and brand applied, the army buttons cut off his clothes—a squad of soldiers with fixed bayonets placed behind him when the band struck up the "rogues' march." The rogue did march all along the line, with hat in hand, a living specimen of the disgraced soldier.

I have concluded not to desert this week at least. . . .

Love to all, hoping to hear from you soon and often.

Ever yours,
JAMES P. COBURN

— ★ —

Robert Goodyear* served as a private with Company B, 27th Connecticut Volunteer Infantry.

Camp of the 27th Reg. C.V. Near Falmouth, Va.
Feb. 14th, 1863

SARAH:

Your kind letter of the 4th reached me a day or two since, and I wait myself of the opportunity to acknowledge and thank you heartily for the same. I should have answered immediately had I not been so busily engaged in building an extension to our little cabin, which connected with the daily routine of camp duties has

*Another letter by Robert Goodyear appears on page 146.

occupied all my time. Nothing affords us so much pleasure in our dreary hours as the kind assurances that our labors, fraught with so many privations and dangers, are duly appreciated by our friends at home.

Yes, the soldier looks upon a letter from home as a perfect God send—sent as it were, by some kind ministering Angel Spirit, to cheer his dark and weary hours. In the present case, I am quite sure none could have been more acceptable than the one from yourself. So, if I fail to do justice of it in the reply, it must be attributed to the nature of circumstances, other than a lack of disposition, for I write now in the position as well as capacity of a soldier and not as teacher of the "Model" Stamp. Hence all defects in orthography, etymology, syntax, and prosody will be entirely overlooked in the all absorbing thought—"it is from a soldier."

And so it should be. In the absence of tables, chairs, the quiet

A scene from daily life in camp

room, etc., the soldier often times gets into the most convenient positions which surrounding circumstances will permit. If he has a portfolio, he will at once seat himself on the nearest billet of wood upon the ground in genuine Ottoman style and commit his thoughts to paper, amid all the noise and confusion incidental to the vast collections and concentration of horses, men, and mules. If he has no portfolio, he will often use the "smooth side of a chip" or make a substitute by folding his blanket and spread himself upon the ground horizontally. And then, too, there is not an hour —not a moment from morning until night, and from night til morn—that is not filled up with Military "Orders," details, etc., together with the unearthly braying of mules and the constant racket of the huge army wagons to which they are attached.

Today I have been detailed, with several others, to guard an ammunition train, so I brought along my portfolio and have seated myself upon a bale of hay to write. Around me are a hundred or more army wagons loaded with powder, shot, and shell. To each wagon is attached six mules, said to have been through the Peninsular Campaign with Gen. McClellan. They are biting and kicking each other as [if] the very D—had got among them.

And here come a dozen white men. One of them has a huge black whip. They are debating when and how they shall flog a negro. I must stop for a moment. Well, it is all over. The negro was tied to a beam, six lashes applied to his bare back by a white man—offense said to be insulting a white man. This is among the "slight interruptions" with which the soldier letter writer meets so often.

Another calling engages my attention just now of a different nature—and to that calling I have devoted all my energies, all my efforts (feeble as they are), and, if need be, my heart's blood upon the altar of my country. It has cost our family great sacrifices already. It may—doubtless will—cost us greater sacrifices before our task shall have been accomplished. But if the people are true and faithful, the end will be glorious and the victory will be complete.

The war presents to me two phases forced upon us by ambitious and designing men. We have very reluctantly engaged in a war rendered more horrible and bloody by the determined obstinacy of our enemies. Simply that our great government may be preserved from treason and anarchy, and fearful too that if not maintained to the letter, and traitors be allowed to overthrow and break asunder ties most sacred—costing our forefathers long years of blood and toil—all the hope and confidence of the world in the capacity of men for self government will be lost, and, that civilization, Christianity, and education (the three grand pillars in the great temple of liberty which our fathers reared on this continent and consecrated by their prayers and tears) will go down and perhaps be followed by a long night of tyranny and barbarism. To save the nation from such a fate is the only true motive which should govern us in this warfare.

There are a few persons in the army who are unflinchingly true to these principles, and who faithfully strive amid all discouragements to lead our armies on to victory. They are pouring out their blood like water on every battlefield wherever they meet the enemy, and they bear the burdens of war uncomplainingly. They are fighting in a holy cause and they are firmly convinced that in the end all will be well. So they struggle on and will continue to do so until the war is ended, whether it results in the overthrow of rebellion or in our own disgrace and defeat. This is one phase of the war, and I believe our cause shall yet triumph.

It may be a long time yet before we shall see any visible signs of victory, but when the end begins to come it will be like the approach of a thunderstorm—dark and furious for the time, but followed by the clear pure atmosphere giving health and vigor to those who inhale it.

The other phase is a dark one. We have in the army a host of unprincipled men who do not really care which way the wind blows. They would like the name of being victorious, but they are not engaged heart and soul in putting down the rebellion. They talk "secession" and their sympathies are just about as strong for one side as the other. In reality they are our enemies.

But what is the worst feature of all—the war is made a vast

scheme for speculation, and thousands upon thousands of these "army" are filling their pockets and building a name and a fortune from our woes and misfortunes of those who fight and fall in the struggle. Looking at the war as it is conducted, it is the most contemptible humbug that ever entered into the imaginations of men. The rebellion is a gigantic one and our enemies are united in their purpose. We are divided and we not only have to fight the Southern army, but we must also fight against popular sentiment at the North. Our enemies know this and they take advantage. They put their best men in power and they display much skill in the planning of their battles.

In the recent Battle of Fredericksburg, our reg. was ordered to the front. They advanced without flinching under a tremendous fire from the rebel batteries, but their guns were of an inferior quality [Austrian rifles] and half of them wo'd not go off at all. So our boys were slaughtered terribly. After the battle was over, our guns were "inspected," condemned, and finally exchanged for better ones [E. Whitney M1861 rifle muskets]. You are familiar with the Banks Expedition. It is a miracle almost that every vessel did not go to the bottom before they reached their destination.

I must not enumerate the humbugs and impositions practiced upon the army and from which we suffer repeated disasters and defeats. The soldier of today has a keen perception. He has been educated for a different calling, and he is not slow to detect the real character of the war as it is conducted. Abused, humbugged, imposed upon and frequently half-starved and sick, he sees himself made a mere tool for political speculators to operate with. Led on to slaughter and defeat by drunken and incompetent officers, he has become disheartened, discouraged, demoralized. But notwithstanding all his trials and discouragements, and much as the rebels boast of repeated victories, they have not today within the limits of their pretended Confederacy a single state where our forces have not a firm and permanent foothold. They are entirely surrounded by land and sea and the circle of their operations is growing smaller and smaller. Slowly but surely the rebellion is drawing to an inglorious end. It remains with the people of the

North to say whether our cause, so noble, so high and holy, shall triumph, or whether after all our efforts it shall fail to bring us great and glorious results. It is my earnest and heartfelt prayer that our patriotism will be sufficient to stand the test, and that our beneficent government may be purged [of] all that is dishonorable and unrighteous.

Will you pardon me for writing so much? [I] have written much that I did not intend to when I began, and left unwritten some things which I intended to write. Please accept my thanks for the kind introduction as well as the letter, and if agreeable, let me hear from you again. Wishing you much prosperity & happiness, I am

Yours,

R. B. GOODYEAR

— ★ —

Edward Hallock Ketcham* served as a second lieutenant with Company A, 120th New York Volunteer Infantry. His letters, along with his brother's, were published in an anthology entitled Fighting Quakers *in 1866.*

Camp near Falmouth, Va.
Feb. 18th, 1863

DEAR MOTHER:

I received a letter from thee and John yesterday, and one from him today. I know, of course, it must come hard to thee to part with him, and be left alone; but, still thee has kind and sympathizing friends, who will do all that they possibly can to make thy hard lot, as I must call it, easy.

Now, perhaps, it will somewhat soften thy grief, if I tell thee that the hardships of war are greatly exaggerated. I have seen men who told awful stories of their sufferings in their campaign before Richmond brought to admit that what they were then enduring

---

*Another letter by Edward Hallock Ketcham appears on page 140.

equaled any suffering they had before met with. Now, I have never yet seen the three consecutive hours, when I suffered either from cold, heat, thirst, or hunger; or much on account of fatigue.

Soldiers, as a rule, like to be heroes; in fact, that brought a large share of them here, and if they don't exaggerate considerably in their letters home, why, their friends would not have a chance to indulge in hero-worship! Thus it comes that wonderful stories are told; and then it is natural to make any transaction of their own as big as possible, to some people; so, the big yarns find their way home. "Never believe but half a traveler tells you" is a pretty safe rule; but when you come to a soldier, why, reject two-thirds and trim the balance.

Doubtless, the wounded and sick have suffered; but I believe the instances where the well soldier has suffered to any great extent are scarce; never from hunger; except, perhaps, when the baggage-trains have been lost or captured. But if we do suffer some, what does it all amount to? Who expects to go through life gathering roses from which the thorns have been plucked? The back should be shaped to the burden.

Mother, to tell the truth, I did cherish a hope that Jack would be disappointed in getting off; but it seems I was disappointed. I hoped this only on thy account; for I believe these times, and this war, call for just such men as he; and, though he is my only brother, and I know full well his value, I would not have had him prove himself not what I thought him, even if, by so doing, he had stayed at home. I wish the necessity were not; but as it is, if he had chosen to stay at home, it would have gone far to prove that he was not worth coming. He may live to return a hero, or, he may die a martyr. But in either event he will have lived and done his duty, and he who, when death looks him in the face, can say, in truth, I have done my duty, has lived a lifetime, though the blood of youth still courses through his veins.

Lovingly, thy son,

EDWARD H. KETCHAM

— ★ —

James Hamner served as a private with Company C, 21st Tennessee Cavalry. His letter, written during the Middle Tennessee Campaign, is an account of his company's operations at Franklin, Tennessee.

Camp near Franklin, Tenn.
April 11th, 1863

MY DEAR MOTHER:

The day before yesterday our Brigade was ordered out with two days' rations and started toward Franklin. They went within about four miles of the town and were surprised by the enemy. The Brigade was marching very quietly along when the enemy suddenly "turned up" and charged our battery. They took the wheels off the guns and threw them in gullies on the side of the road. We had one regiment in the front and one in the rear of the battery, but everything was so unexpected that they could not get in position until the enemy had done considerable damage. Our battery surrendered immediately but was soon recaptured by our troops. As soon as they saw that we were going to retake it, they shot the Captain of the battery through the head, killing him instantly. It was the most outrageous thing I ever heard of. He was one of the best artillerists in the service and a noble, kind-hearted man. His name was Freeman from Nashville. I was not along as I had to remain with the ordnance wagons.

At the time, we were (that is, our Brigade) on the Franklin and Lewisburg Pike. Gen. Van Dorn went up on the Columbia and Franklin Pike. I think it was the intention to take Franklin, but it was a failure. Gen. Van Dorn got into the town but was not able to hold it. He fought them about half an hour, but had to leave, as he was too weak to hold it. We lost several in killed and wounded, but they lost more than we did. Gen. Van Dorn had his horse killed under him at Franklin. I hear today that they are fighting in or near Shelbyville. I suppose Gen. Johnson and Rosecrans have both advanced. If that be the case, we will soon know whether we will hold this country or not. I hope we may be able to stay here, but if we are not, you all must not be discouraged, as it is our policy to lose as few men as possible. There is no use in fighting unless we can accomplish something by it. I think we have one of the best armies in the world, but still if they outnumber us too far, we must not fight them, for when the army we have now is gone, I cannot see where the next one is to come from. Our forces now outnumber the men we had at Murfreesboro by about fifteen thousand as far as I can learn, but the enemy has been strongly reinforced in the last month. There is no one in the Confederacy that would hate to fall back worse than I would, but still I have such confidence in our officers that I will not grumble at anything they do. If we leave Tullahoma, we will fall back to the mountains or Bridgeport on the Tenn. River. If we go to Bridgeport, they can never move us from there, unless they flank us. I trust we will not have to fall back, as this is the best country we will find to stay in. Tell the young ladies (if we do fall back) that they must not grumble, as Gen. Johnson has an eye to them and does not wish to have all the young men killed, as he wishes to leave them all a husband when we have peace again. I am very anxious to see the end of this war to see what course things will take in our government.

I notice a disposition on the part of some of our leading politicians and some of the newspapers to spring a new revolution before this one is closed. Some of them are advancing the property qualification for voters after this war is over. Such men are not friends to the Confederacy. A writer in the *Southern Literary Messenger*, published at Richmond, uses the following language: "We sadly need, too, a property qualification for native as well as foreign. It is hardly necessary to repeat the trite argument of the greater interestedness of the property holders in the successful administration of the Government, than of him who has nothing at stake." I think that such articles as this should be kept from the eyes of our troops, at any rate until the war is over, for it does no good and I know of one man who deserted, on the belief that such would be our policy hereafter. For my part I do not fear that such will be the policy of our Government, as it would certainly create another revolution, but there is plenty of men who do think so and who will act on that belief and desert the army. In conclusion the writer said: "Finally, we should curtail the number of officers elective by the people. These, and we might suggest others, are some of the features in our social organism which have occurred to us as sadly needing alteration." He wished the President to have the power to appoint a large number of officers, and thereby create a central power, the very thing to guard against. If we would have an educational qualification then we might do better, but such is not the policy of our leading men, as there is too many men who own property that cannot read and write. Let every man be made to sign his name when he goes to the polls to deposit his vote and then the name of the man he votes for—that is my doctrine. Well, as this is most too early a day to begin talking of such things, I shall stop it.

Tell Mr. Alford I am getting tired of the army, and would like to help him fish this summer, but fear I will have other fish to fry. Direct your letters to Columbia as the Yanks have not got it yet.

— ★ —

When he wrote this letter home, Major Thomas Elder was serving as an officer of commissary and subsistence to Brigadier General Roger Pryor. Before this appointment, he had served with the 3rd Virginia Volunteer Infantry. His letter was written four days after the Confederate victory at the Battle of Chancellorsville, Virginia.

Subsistence Dept., Perry's Brigade
Camp near Fredericksburg
May 8th, '63

MY DEAR WIFE:

Only yesterday I mailed you a letter from Guiney's Station, but as Lt. Taylor of Genl. Perry's staff goes to Richmond tomorrow, I send this by him to be mailed in that city, hoping it will reach you sooner than do most of my letters delivered to the post up here.

Yesterday we returned to our old camp after an absence of just one week—a week full of events, and fraught, I trust, with much good to our country.

The enemy has been badly, ignominiously whipped, at a time and upon ground of his own choosing, and driven back over the river in disgrace. Genl. Lee's infantry force did not exceed forty-five thousand muskets, and his troops of all arms did not probably reach sixty thousand. The enemy's force, it is believed, was doubly as large as ours. Moreover, we were not expecting an attack; our artillery was far in the rear, whither it had been sent to procure forage for the horses. Never, in all probability, will the enemy have such another opportunity in Virginia.

The camp of the 150th Pennsylvania Infantry, March 1863

Our men fought splendidly; there was no straggling, and each soldier seemed to feel that he had an important part to act in the grand and bloody drama. The enemy's infantry fought badly, did not stand our charges and seemed willing to surrender the content. His artillery was served with his usual skill and efficiency. Hooker, the great braggart and last pet of the Yankee nation, has been crushed, ruined, and must now give place to some other man.

Meanwhile, our own great Lee continues to grow in the confidence and esteem of our soldiers and people. Our troops idolize him, and as for myself, I cannot find terms adequate to express my admiration of him. I wish you could see him; he presents such a calm, dignified, benevolent appearance. It has been said of him by English correspondents that he is a man whom children would instinctively select in a crowd as one who was their friend. I think this remark conveys a very good idea of the man. He is, beyond doubt, much the ablest man engaged on either side in this war. With his comparatively small force, the enemy pressed him both at Chancellorsville and at Fredericksburg; yet he managed both forces with entire ease and succeeded in driving them both entirely across the river and came very near capturing the whole force at Fredericksburg. We have probably seven thousand prisoners.

I expect much good from this fight. I think the Yankees and the rest of mankind must soon come to the conclusion that the South cannot be subjugated. This last defeat—the greatest sustained by the enemy during the war—must greatly strengthen the hands of the large peace party at the North who maintain that fighting will never settle the difficulties between two sections; and tend to induce foreign powers to recognize us as an independent nation, inasmuch as it goes towards demonstrating our capacity to defend ourselves. I am very anxious to see the Yankee newspapers and am anxious to know how they take their defeat, what conclusions they deduce from it, etc.

It is gratifying to me to know that, in my humble way, I have done my duty. My brigade received their rations regularly without missing a meal during the whole week of the battles. I am glad to know I am serving my country with some degree of usefulness in this, her hour of trial. To have served during the war in Genl. Lee's army is indeed, in my estimation, a subject of honest pride, and though I may leave my children poor in worldly goods, it is gratifying to know they will be able to speak of their father as one of the soldiers of the second revolution for Independence. . . .

Genl. Jackson was at last accounts doing well. His wife is with him at a house near Guiney's Station. Besides having his left arm amputated between the elbow and shoulder, he has a bullet hole through the palm of his right hand. He is quite cheerful. He and Genl. A. P. Hill were both shot, through mistake, by our own men. The latter received only a slight wound.

Our brigade fought well and lost in killed and wounded about 125. A lieutenant of my acquaintance in the brigade was shot in the arm on Sunday morning, had it amputated near the shoulder the same evening, and the next day I met him walking ten miles from the battlefield and as cheerful as ever. He walked to Guiney's Station, distance twenty-two miles from the battlefield, the same evening, sat down to our table, ate a hearty supper, and the following day went on to Richmond. Wasn't he a hero?

Do write to me every mail. Believe me, as ever, my dear wife,

Your fondly devoted husband,
THOS. C. ELDER

— ★ —

On the Federal side, Edward Hallock Ketcham,* a second lieutenant with Company A, 120th New York Volunteer Infantry, wrote home to give an account of the Union defeat at Chancellorsville.

———

Camp Near Falmouth, [Va.]
May 12th, 1863

MY DEAR MOTHER:

I wrote to thee from the battlefield, after we had come out of the fight, and telegraphed to thee again after we had recrossed the

———

*Another letter by Edward Hallock Ketcham appears on page 133.

river. If thee received either, I, of course, do not know; but I will repeat the vital part of both.

Jack and I are close together once more; both well and hearty. This old camp was, during last winter, a pleasant place. Winter has gone, and the quiet and repose that were then not only endurable but somewhat pleasant are so no longer; and I shall be truly glad when we shall leave it for good; I can bid good bye to the old log cabin without regret.

Mother, the short campaign, which we have just passed through, was one of hardship; but, to me, its hardest experience was mere play; I am able to stand just such, for six months, without inconvenience. God help the army of the Potomac, if we are ever so hard-worked that I give out; for there are few that can stand the pressure after that.

Mother, this time spent here is not lost time—I mean I personally sacrifice nothing. I have often thought that old age that has

Assistant adjutant general officer and staff in camp, Falmouth, Virginia

no experience of hardship or adventure to fall back on, when the time comes that we live in the past as I now do in the future, must be somewhat barren. If I come out all right and do not fail to do my duty, just the experience of the last nine months I would not part with for all the wealth of New York City.

It is commonly thought that a soldier's life is rather calculated to demoralize. I do not believe it. It may appear so on the surface; but there is many a man here in this army who has never thought a serious thought before who thinks now, and, when he goes back to home and friends, he will go back to realize that there is something for him to live for besides himself. *It does men good to suffer for a good cause.* It somehow identifies them with it; and, as one good cause is linked with everything else that is good and noble, a man in fighting for liberty somehow fights his way to goodness. The general effect on the men here will be humanizing, and with peace—an honorable one, as we mean to win—will come national virtue.

It is a tough sight, for one who looks only on the surface, to see the noblest and the bravest of the land limping and bleeding and dying, as I saw them on the field of battle. But when you look upon a man who died stoutly doing his duty and can realize that he died to save something better than life, it does not seem so awful as it would. It was an awful picture we looked upon the other day; but it had a bright as well as a dark side. There were many brave men who saw the last of earth on that battlefield of Chancellorsville, and many tears will flow, for many a year. But what are these tears to the bitter ones a mother sheds over an erring son, out of whom everything good has died, and only his body lives?

If we were whipped at Chancellorsville, as the Copperheads say we were, I think such getting whipped, on our part, will soon use up the Confederacy. Their loss must have been fearful; for they came up, time after time, right in front of our batteries, closed en masse, and were just let to come close enough, when our guns, double-shotted with grape, would pile them in heaps, and send them back, utterly cut to pieces. This was not only one occurrence, but it was done over and over again. But I must stop.

Affectionately, thy son,
EDWARD H. KETCHAM

Edward Ketcham was killed in action at the Battle of Gettysburg on July 2, 1863.

— ★ —

John Lewis, a private serving with Company D, 17th Connecticut Volunteer Infantry, also wrote home to give an account of the Federal defeat at Chancellorsville.

———

Brooks Station, Va.
May 14th, 1863

MY DEAR WIFE:

I have wrote you two letters since I came out of the field of battle. I am as well as can be expected after our long and tiresome march. We have a great many missing out of our company, which makes the rest of us feel very lonesome. There is a great many officers of our regiment resigning. Capt. Lucy of our company has resigned and gone home. The company called him a coward and we told him that we hoped that the folks at home would treat him as such.

Augusta, I never expected to live to write you again when on the battlefield, for the Rebel bullets came down like a shower of hail stones all around me. When we had orders to lay down, we was in a garden supporting the 13th N.Y. Battery. The Rebels came down upon us by thousands and poured an awful volley of grape and canister into our ranks, but it passed over our heads.

When the Lt. Col. gave us orders to retreat, we got up and we rallied around our colors at the next rifle pit. Col. Noble was wounded while giving us orders to stand firm. The Lt. Col. was killed in the garden. We got most of the regiment together, but the Rebels came down on us with such great numbers that we broke and fell back on the line of the 12th Corps.

As I was running, the Rebel balls came around me like hail stones and I thought I should have to be taken prisoner. I was completely exhausted from running so far so I got down behind a large pine tree to keep from getting shot. I had no sooner got behind the tree when a shell burst within six feet of me, plowing and rooting up the ground and cutting down the brush all around me. . . .

Our regiment was now scattered all over, but I had not gone far when I fell in with Harry Glipp. We went on together till we came to the 107th N.Y. Regiment. The Rebs was now gaining on us, but the 11th and 12th Corps was all mixed in together. We formed in line of battle and fired a volley into the Rebel ranks, which made them stagger. Our artillery then opened on them, which dealt destruction in their ranks at every fire and checked them. Then they was glad to fall back. It was now ten o'clock Saturday night.

They did not trouble us anymore that night, so we lay down on our arms waiting for them to make their appearance and thinking of the past fight and of the dreadful Sunday that was coming and of our comrades that had fallen and I prayed for you all at home and thanked God that my life was spared to write to you and perhaps to meet you again.

As soon as morning came, our batteries opened on the Rebs and shelled the woods. They had now massed all of their force together, and on they came, but were mowed down like grass by our infantry and artillery and piled up in heaps three deep. The fight lasted about four hours when firing ceased, and we now organized the regiments and each man went to his regiment. The 11th and 12th Corps was now relieved by the 2nd and 5th Corps, and we were sent to the left and placed on the breastworks, where we stayed for three days in a drenching rain.

On the 6th, in the morning about three o'clock, we were ordered in line of march. We marched to the United States Ford, where we found all of the army crossing on the pontoons. Our regt. crossed about ten o'clock.

We are all back on this side of the Rappahannock. It has been an awful blow to the Rebs. Hooker gained his point and if General Sedgwick had held his position on Fredericksburg Heights, we would be within a few miles of Richmond today, but he was too ambitious and advanced too far and the Rebs flanked him and he had to re-cross the river.

Oh, Augusta, if I could only sit down and relate to you the sights that I have seen of the field of battle. It is enough to break the stoutest heart to hear the cries and groans of the wounded and dying. There was a young man named Wm. Clark in our company that was wounded. As we were retreating, he was shot in the groin. The blood was flowing from him, covering the ground. He saw me as I was passing him and he called on me to help him. He said he was shot and could go no farther. I took and laid him over on a little green mound, said goodbye and left him. I could not stay with him and would have been shot or taken prisoner. I had to leave, but I guess the poor fellow is dead and out of all misery. . . .

Give my love to all at home and receive a thousand kisses for yourself and give a number to the little ones for me. I must now close, may God protect you.

Write soon,

JOHN

John Lewis died on March 11, 1864, at Beaufort, South Carolina.

— ★ —

Robert Goodyear* served as a sergeant with Company B, 27th Connecticut Volunteer Infantry.

U.S. Hospital
Convalescent Camp, Va.
May 30, 1863

MY DEAR FRIEND:

Your kind letter of the 5th, owing to the frequent changes to which we have been subjected of late, did not reach me until day before yesterday. I am sorry to say that it did not find me in health, as was the case when I wrote to you some time ago, but it is a part of the soldier's experience to meet with reverses, be it untold fatigue, exposures in the field, wounds, etc. And thank our Heavenly Father for the kind preserving care He has bestowed upon

Ward K at the Armory Square Hospital, Washington, D.C.

*Another letter by Robert Goodyear appears on page 128.

myself and so many of my comrades during the weary and bloody campaign thro which we have recently passed.

I suppose you have heard before this of the series of battles fought at and near Fredericksburg, of our capture and imprisonment in Richmond, and of our return as "paroled prisoners of war." I would like to write you a sketch of our experience during the recent campaign. It is one of painful interest but at present I must dismiss all thoughts of exercise, mental or physical, for I am in the hospital and entirely confined to my bed. I have been here nearly a week and—having a fever—hope the most severe part of the fever is over, for I feel very much relieved. The fatigue, exposures and the food which we have been obliged to eat have proved too much for me.

Yes you have "come at last!" A happy greeting to you! Would that it were really yourself, for the presence of a familiar face and a "delicate step"—to say nothing of the soft hand and kind words in a place like this, where there are so many sick—would do more towards alleviating the sufferings of the sick than all the doctors' medicines. Am not I making quite a concession for an "old bach"? Well, you see I am not one of that hardened kind who believe in the stoical doctrine of "total disregard of the sex," but on the other hand am rather an admirer of their many excellent qualities and womanly virtues. And, really, tho I have heard and read of so many being "taken in" and have been "gently admonished" and repeatedly warned of approaching danger, still I have never suffered any "uncomfortable apprehensions" from their presence and familiarity, but in the event of such a circumstance as that to which you allude, I don't know what effect it might have on my poor brain. Perhaps I might "evaporate" like a comet, or turn into a "Sack of Salt" like Lot's wife. At any rate there would undoubtedly be a "Sack" to it. Well, don't be alarmed! I have been "under fire" and stood the test of lightning and hail, blood, thunder, and bomb shells, and if I can stand these, why have I not good reason to hope that I might so survive the dangers and perils of the "ordeal" of which your letter is suggestive? [I] rather think I'm on the safe side yet. . . .

On our "march" from Richmond to Petersburg, Va., we were caught in a terrible thunderstorm, followed by heavy rain and darkness almost impenetrable. We were 8 or 10 miles from Petersburg. The rebs intended to have marched us there the same night. It was then about 9 or 10 o'clock P.M. There were some 2000 of us, floundering along in the mud, and bumping each other at every step. One of our boys was trampled on by a horse of one of the rebel officers. It soon became evident that we could not proceed, and still more evident that we would not, for the boys conceived a very sudden passion for rest, and took to the woods on each side of the way with a natural instinct, and in a half an hour we were all rolled up in our blankets, scattered promiscuously over the ground for a distance of a half mile each way or more, not knowing or caring whether it was raining or not. I must say sleep to me that night was as sweet as I ever enjoyed, tho undoubtedly it had much to do in bringing me where I am. I know it seems strange, but it is never the less true that the soldier will become so exhausted and weary that he will repose quietly and sleep soundly where bullets are whistling by him like storms of hail, and where the thunder of cannon is filling the air with bursting shell, and where the shot are plugging above and around him. I have seen this illustrated several times.

"Copperheads" thick there? Ah! that is one great trouble with us at the north, and if we fail at last, it will be for want of united effort. It is lamentable that we have such an opposition to contend with at home while our trials and hardships are so severe in the field. They ought to know that our cannon and bayonets are the only safeguards between their liberties and their subjugation. A few months' experience in the Jeff Davis Gov't would cure many of the Secession croakers, I fancy. They are too cowardly to fight and too unprincipled to appreciate the efforts of those who are doing and daring everything to lead the nation on to success and victory. But why waste our breath over them? History will assign them an "appropriate sphere," and doubtless give them all the credit which their conduct entitles them to.

At present, all our hope of immediate success hinges upon the efforts of Gen. Grant at Vicksburg. We gained a glorious victory at Fredericksburg recently but lost it again in a very short time. While we were fighting them in the rear, a part of our forces took the heights at Fredericksburg—their Gibralter of the Rappahannock—from which they slaughtered our forces so fearfully on that memorable Dec. 13th. But in their haste to form a junction with Gen. Hooker, whom Gen. Jackson was threatening in the rear, they left too small a force to guard the positions gained, and thus we lost a great advantage—the very key to Richmond by the Rappahannock route.

It does seem that victory is not destined to crown the efforts of the Potomac Army. And I can attribute it to no other reason than to the corruption and wickedness existing in it. Still will we hope on—trusting and praying that God in His own good time will give us the victory and crown our efforts with an honorable and permanent peace. . . . But I have already written more than I expected to when I began. And so I must ask you to consider when you read the contents of this that it is from an "invalid," and with my kindest wishes, with the hope of receiving another favor from you, will sign myself,

Your Friend
R. B. Goodyear

— ★ —

John Townsend Ketcham served as a second lieutenant with Company M, 4th New York Cavalry. The following letter describes the death of his brother, Edward Hallock Ketcham,* at the Battle of Gettysburg, July 2, 1863.

Frederick City
July 8th, 1863

Dear Mother:

I telegraphed to thee as soon as I could, and wrote about Edward. I cannot realize that he is dead. Don't let it kill thee, mother! Thee and I are all that is left of us.

*Letters by Edward Ketcham appear on pages 133 and 140.

Edward was the first man killed in the regiment. They were lying on the ground, behind a little mill, in front of our batteries, making a part of the outer line of battle. It is always necessary in such time for someone to keep a lookout to watch the movements of the enemy. As the men all lay on their faces, Edward was sitting up to look; a sharpshooter's bullet probably struck him in the temple, and went through his head. He put up his hand, and said: "Oh!" and fell on his elbow, quite dead.

There was heavy fighting on the ground soon after, and our forces had possession of the field for a short time. Ed's body was carried back a couple of hundred yards, and left under a tree. I heard of it the next morning, and went to the regiment, and got a man to go with me, who helped to carry him off; he showed me where he lay. It was outside of our breastworks forty or fifty yards, and a couple of hundred beyond our outer line of sharpshooters. I went out to them, but could not get beyond; for a bullet would whistle by, the moment a man showed himself.

I lay down behind a big rock. Whilst I lay there, two rebel batteries commenced to play on ours. I never imagined such a thunder as the firing made; there were twenty-four cannon at work, and the shells burst over our heads, fifty feet or more; one or two men were hurt near me, and the limbs of the trees dropped occasionally. I then took a musket, thinking I would stay with the infantry, till they advanced, as I was not needed with the department, it being with the mule train; the rest of our regiment was at Washington.

Pretty soon the rebels came out from their works, in heavy force, and advanced in line. Our batteries commenced to mow them down, and the men lay down until in close range; then the outer line raised up, and the two lines fought, without either moving from their place. It was a grand, but terrible sight! The rebels concentrated on one part of our line, and pressed it back, to charge our breastworks; our flanks closed in on them, and hundreds were driven in, prisoners, while the rest ran back to their lines like sheep. One poor fellow came in just by me; the first words he said were, "Gentlemen, I do this because I am forced to."

I went out at night, to look for Edward, but could not find him. The next morning our line advanced, and I went out to the tree; and there, on his back, his hands peacefully on his breast, lay all that was left of the brother I have lived so closely with all my life. His features, though discolored and swollen, had an expression I have seen on them before—peaceful rest. He had lain thirty-six hours on the field, with the roaring of cannon and bursting of shells over him, and the feet of contending hosts, of darkness and freedom, trampling the ground he lay on.

When I got him, I brought him down under a tree. A Captain of one of the batteries said to me, "If he were a brother of mine, I would bury him on the field of glory." He was very kind, and sent me men to dig the grave. In a little grove behind the batteries, under an oak tree, in his soldier's uniform, wrapped in a shelter-tent, lies all the earthly remains of my brother. "He has gone to be a soldier in the army of the Lord." And mother, thee and I walk this world of sorrow.

I set for his head-stone a piece of a young oak cut off by a rebel shell, and marked his name and regiment.

Mother, yet a little time thee and I have to walk this earth, when we compare it to the great eternity beyond, where father and Edward are gone before us.

Oh, he was cut down in the very morning of his manhood! He is laid a sacrifice on the altar of Liberty!

He died to give to every other man the right to his own man-hood—a precious sacrifice—for in him were heroism, a brave heart, and an iron will. He died as he would have died—with his face toward the enemies of freedom, on the battlefield.

Edward has marched many a weary mile; he has lain on the wet, cold ground, with nothing over him, long nights, with the rain pouring on him, and never murmured; he has lain and shiv-ered in the snow and slush, all long winter nights, after weary marches, hungry, perhaps, or after eating a few hard crackers, and a little raw meat; and, in his discomfort, he has never wished for home; except, perhaps, to look forward to that bright day when the rebellion would be crushed, and he should return home, war-worn, and covered with his well worn honors. That day, alas! he can never see. Oh, God! Thy price for freedom is a *dear one*!

JOHN

Shortly afterward, John Ketcham was taken prisoner by the Confederates and sent to Libby Prison, where he died on October 8, 1863.

— ★ —

Florence McCarthy served as a chaplain for the 7th Virginia Volunteer Infantry.

———

Williamsport, Maryland
July 10, 1863

DEAR SISTER:

I saw Billy a few days ago. He was cheerful and in excellent health and said that Julian was well as usual.

They were in the hottest of the battle. Jim Marpin and another young man were shot through and through by a cannon ball at Billy's gun.

Williamsport is a one-horse town on the north bank of the Potomac and in the western part of the valley. The houses are riddled and almost all deserted, and the country for a mile around is fetid with beef offal and dead horses. We passed through this place on our way north, went from here to Hagerstown and then to Greencastle, Pa., Chambersburg, Pa., Gettysburg, Pa.—where we fought—and then to Hagerstown, Maryland, and Williamsport, Maryland, again. At the present Ewell's Corps is at Hagerstown, Picket's Division is here, and I have no conception where the remainder of the army is unless it has gone to Boonsboro or Sharpsburg.

I have been marched nearly to death. In coming from Gettysburg here, we marched three days and two nights without stopping except long enough to cook food. Most of the time it rained and the roads were perfectly awful. My socks have given out, I can buy none, beg none, steal none and it is a matter of impossibility to get a piece of clothing washed. I am lousy and dirty and have no hope of changing flannel for weeks to come. Food has been scarcer than ever. We are now enjoying a resting spell, which has already lasted three days.

We passed through Berryville, Virginia. The ladies were very kind and polite to the soldiers, but appeared to me to be rich, unrefined and ugly and ill-favored generally. Williamsport is a nest of abolitionists and free negroes. Hagerstown shut up the windows and put on mourning when we came, but when the Yankee prisoners came through went into ecstasies. Greencastle is a pretty place of about two hundred inhabitants connected by railroad with Chambersburg. Chambersburg is a pretty little city of six thousand inhabitants. I could not get into Gettysburg. It was torn all to pieces with shell.

In all these places, the Confederate authority opened the stores and compelled the merchants to sell their stocks to the soldier at the regular prices and for Confederate money. But the advanced troops, as usual, got all the plunder. All I could buy was a few buttons and a pair of misses' stockings, which I have worn out. I got stuff for a pair of pants in Williamsport for eight dollars. The last suit Mrs. Cook made for me is coming all to flinders. The lining busts every time the wind blows. My pants in particular are believed to be in a blue way.

Some few of the Pennsylvania people in town showed some spirits. One old woman beat our men out of her garden with a stick. A girl in Chambersburg took water and a broom and washed the pavement where our men had laid their haversacks. But as a general thing, they are the most cringing mean-spirited people on earth. I saw one with his son dragging sticks of wood out of the road so that our troops could march better. They tell us that they are sorry for us being in a strange land, and are willing to do all they can for us. They will do anything to save property or their hides. The women are all gross and sinewy. The men speak of them invariably as "the women" and say they have no ladies here. The country is fine naturally and is highly cultivated and very productive. The crops surprised our soldiers, but are only half crops, they say, for that section.

Our men have strict orders to take nothing without paying, but they do just as they please, which is not a twentieth part as bad as they did in Virginia. The chickens, hogs and vegetables are being consumed rapidly. The crop in some places will be ruined by camps and by stock, but we have not hurt them enough to talk about. All their public property except state property has been destroyed that we could destroy.

Stereoscopic photographs of the body of a

The Battle of Gettysburg was the most awful of the war, but the battle proper did not last three hours. Our division is thought to have suffered most. It has been detailed a provost errand for the army, so small has it been made. I'm inclined to think, however, that it will be kept in the field and compelled in the future as in the past to do the hardest marching and the hardest fighting of the war.

Colonel Patton, it was thought, was killed. Colonel Flowers has been reinstated and has taken command. He is the most immodest, obscene, profane, low flung blackguard on the earth and hates me with a perfect hatred. I do not believe I have another enemy in the regiment but him. He had tried his best last year to disgrace and ruin me and I expect now he will try harder than ever. I shall not

Confederate soldier at Little Round Top, Gettysburg

be surprised at anything he does. My plan is to keep cool, say
nothing and suffer everything. . . .

Give my best love to pa and ma and all.

Your affectionate brother,

F. McCarthy

— ★ —

At the time of writing, Edwin Fay was serving as a sergeant
with the Minden Rangers. His letter was written following the
Second Vicksburg Campaign, which lasted from April 29–July
4, 1863.*

Camp 4 miles in rear Mechanicsburg
July 10th, 1863

My own dear Wife:

I wrote you a long letter yesterday but on sober reflection last
night while all the Camps were wrapped in sleep I concluded that
it was too wicked to send you and I have concluded this morning
to write again. I have little indeed to write as news is scarce in this
part of the Country. Vicksburg as you will already have heard has
been surrendered to the enemy and 17,500 brave Southern men
have laid down their arms and given up the stronghold, the key
of the Confederacy.† It is almost impossible to tell the consequences but if Grant is wise Port Hudson will fall in less than a
week and then Mobile, Selma, Montgomery, Atlanta, Augusta,
Charleston. There is one escape and I am almost in hopes that
Grant will pursue Johnston to Jackson as we learned yesterday
that they were skirmishing at Clinton halfway between Jackson
and Vicksburg. If we can keep them from Port Hudson till we can
get there we may prevent such a series of disasters. God only
knows what will be the fate of the Confederacy. I believe that as

---

*Other letters by Edwin Fay appear on pages 47 and 52.

†Fay underestimated the number of Confederates taken at Vicksburg; 2,166
officers and 27,230 enlisted men surrendered to Grant's forces on July 4.

a power of the Earth it is conquered, but do not near believe the people are subjugated. I have little hope of the future.

But as an offset we hear of the total discomfiture of the Yankee Army in Maryland 12 miles from Baltimore at the Relay House some 30 miles north of Washington, having killed 4 Brig Gen'ls and severely wounded Col. Mead, the successor of Hooker in command of the largest army on the Planet. Washington will doubtless be captured. Such being the case I have a faint hope that a compromise of some kind will be effected which may result in Peace. This is a faint hope but drowning men will catch at straws, you know. The Yankee troops were told that when Vicksburg was taken they would be paid off, discharged, and go home, that peace would be made at once. Poor deluded, miserable wretches to believe a lie. How many thousands of their bones will bleach beneath a Southern sun ere they will see the dawn of peace. If Johnston whips Grant, as he will if he can fight him outside his entrenchments, the Yankee glory will be shortlived. God grant that he may get the opportunity.

Johnston was moving to relieve Pemberton and the time of the attack was to have been July 7th and Pemberton surrendered on the 4th, alleging starvation as the cause. The 10th was agreed upon and the blame rests on Pemberton. Thus we have suffered from Southern men of Northern birth. New Orleans, Vicksburg, and the Confederacy all gone unless by a direct interposition of Providence. We hear that New Orleans is in our hands but it won't be long if Grant moves down the River. But a truce to War Matters, though a word more. I very much fear you will be visited by the Vandals before long, for I know there is a lack of ammunition on the west side of the river and if so you may look for me home. I may come anyhow. I can't tell you, you need not be surprised to see me at almost any time. I feel sad to think that all my sufferings and toils are all lost to the Country all in vain. My first allegiance is to my family, my second to my Country.

Mr. Minchew came last Friday but he brought me no letter from you. Others had received letters from Minden by mail since Caufield's return there, some as late as 19th but none for me and you can imagine how I felt. Tuesday I got yours of the 16th inst. and you don't know how rejoiced I was to get it, but at the same time I thought it was very tame and cool considering I had not had a letter for nearly two months. I thought it not an equivalent for the long letters overflowing with my heart's warmest love I had sent you weekly save on the march from Tenn. I can very readily see how you, surrounded with friends and supplied with your heart's desires, can feel or rather cannot realize the longing, yearning for loving words of those who are deprived of every comfort, cut off from friends and even intelligence of home. I know you thought your letter everything that could be desired and in fact it was quite a friendly letter, not more, and I think I ought to expect something more than friendship from my wife. You promised to write a long letter the next Saturday but I shall never get it I fear as everything is in such confusion now and I expect this is the last letter you will get from me unless I write by Minchew and there is no telling when he will start as he is trying to get a discharge for Gus and that may take him two months to get his papers through. . . . .

If some terms of accommodation are not come to between the contending powers, this will be a war of extermination. I cannot keep from the War Theme, my pen is like Anacreon's lyre only its strains instead of those of Cupid belong rather to Mars bristling with his helmet and shield. I wish you to keep that pistol loaded and capped and if the Yankees come to Minden to wear it on your person, never be without it and the first one that dares insult you blow his brains out. This you must do or you are not the woman I married. I expect to murder every Yankee I ever meet when I can do so with impunity if I live a hundred years and peace is made in six months. Peace will never be made between me and any Yankee if I can kill him without too great risk. The Thugs of India will not bear a comparison to my hatred and destruction of them when opportunity offers. There can be no fellowship between us forever. I wish you were in Mexico. I would not be long in joining you and we would seek some abode in a South American state, but that climate would be unhealthy for Yankees as long as I stayed there.

I expect to send this letter by a Mr. Underwood of Harrison's Co. who will cross at Helena. He says he was in sight there the other day and saw our Guns playing fog with Yanks' transports, though he is not a very reliable character and may have been mistaken. I hope he will get this letter across for me somewhere. I have written you a good many things lately that I wanted done but I don't know whether or not you have had them done. You wrote me something once upon a time about my hogs dying with cholera but did not tell me if we had any left at all nor one word about our cattle. I could never tell from your letters that we had ever kept house or had anything, whether we lived in a city or country, but I suppose you have so much to do in school that you have no time to think of these things.

The report has just come in that Bragg has fallen back to the Tenn. River, Rosecrans having whipped him or rather flanked him and caused him to fall back. If it had not been for Bragg's incompetency we would have held possession of all of Ky. and Tenn. We have been thoroughly blessed with incompetents in this Western Dept. Jeff Davis thinks Richmond is Heaven or nearly so while the loss of Vicksburg is incomparably greater than 40 such cities as Richmond, yet the latter has been surrendered, the former held.

I am glad to learn that Thornwell is talking so plainly and glad too that his memory is so good. I recollect making him eat a crust and I presume it has been kept alive in his memory by Laura and others. Bless him, he bids fair to be as intelligent as our darling eldest born. Oh this accursed, infernal war, how I wish it could be closed now on some terms. I want to see my wife and child, they are a necessity to me altho I may not be to them. I *must come home.* Of course you have had the wagon fixed for Thornwell? I am very much afraid your being in school has proved much to his detriment and I fear you do not govern him as rigidly as you ought, for he may be left to your sole control and management through life unassisted except it be by a stepfather. Poor child, his lot will then be a hard one, for I have not seen a man since I have been in the army save one that was worthy the love of a good woman. . . .

But I must close my letter, I know it is not interesting but it is the best I can do under the circumstances. I am glad to hear that you have so much flour. I wish we could get some, for this corn-bread will sour in 12 hours and we are required to keep 2 days' rations on hand all the time. But I must write to Mother a hasty note to let her know I have not been surrendered at Vicksburg, for she will worry if she does not hear. I want to write to Spencer too before long as I expect he is now in Chattanooga. I am tired of this eternal state of suspense. Whatever is to be done I want it done quickly. My love to your Mother, Father and Sisters. What did your Father go to Shreveport for? Don't let him neglect that matter of Spencer's. Good Bye, dearest.

Your husband
E. H. Fay

— ★ —

David Wyatt Aiken served as colonel with the 7th South Carolina Infantry. This letter to his wife is an account of the Confederate defeat at the Battle of Gettysburg, Pennsylvania, July 1–3, 1863. In this most crucial battle of the war, the Confederate Army suffered 28,063 casualties.

Near Hagerstown
July 11th, 1863

Well, my dearest wife, I wrote you a hurried note in pencil about three days ago, but doubt if it has ever yet crossed the Potomac, and even if it has, I know your joy in seeing my hand-writing once more will be such that you will willingly read a reiteration of the contents of my former letter.

Well, to begin anew at our first crossing of the Potomac. This was done in the rain on the 26th June. And by the way, this is the only dry day we have had since, or the only day we have not had either heavy dews or rains. We marched reasonably along through

Hagerstown, Middleburg, Greencastle, Chambersburg, here taking the right to Cashtown thence to Gettysburg, where we first met the enemy, one and a half miles before reaching the city. Our army, as I wrote you, moved left in front, Ewell's Corps leading the way, and going north from Chambersburg, towards Harrisburg, as far as Carlisle, while Hill and Longstreet went towards Gettysburg.

On the 1st July Hill met the enemy, fought and whipped him, driving him two miles beyond Gettysburg to some very high hills or barren mountains, as formidable as Gibraltar. The next night and day Ewell swung around southeast, marching towards Gettysburg, and we moved to the right of Hill, all the army being in line of battle by noon of the 2nd, confronting the enemy with a line running almost due north and south, and perhaps 15 or more miles long. About noon the cannonading began, and at 2 P.M. we were ordered to advance with the infantry, which we did in fine style directly in front of the cannon not 1,000 yds. distant, which immediately began playing on Kershaw's Brigade, the most exposed having to advance from behind the stone wall just in the edge of the woods through a large level clover field. Just before we moved a shell struck my color guard, killing two men and wounding three. We moved up though, quietly, not able to shoot a gun for some time. Presently we came upon the infantry, the artillery retiring, and then we went at it in earnest. We fought for [a] half hour or more, and drove the enemy for half a mile perhaps, and during my experience I have never seen so much damage done both parties in so short a space of time. I had 18 men killed, several mortally wounded, and about 100 more or less wounded, some 20 only stunned by shells who have already reported for duty. My Regt. suffered about as all the other Regts. in the Brigade. Sixteen of my men have lost arms or legs. That night we lay on the battlefield, and next morning by daylight were ordered to advance amid the groans of the wounded enemy (ours had been moved back) and over the dead of both parties. We found the enemy had retired to the sides of the rocky mountain, in our front, and had themselves so fortified we could do nothing with [the] infantry.

During the fight of the two days we captured about 11,000 prisoners.

On the morning of the 3rd Genl. Lee ordered Genl. Pickett (a Virg. Division that had not been engaged) to attack the most vulnerable portion of the enemy's line, while he shelled their entire line with artillery. Our general line of infantry were then withdrawn to the woods from which we had driven the enemy, about midway between the enemy's and our line. Here we lay down when the cannonading began. We opened 175 cannons at one time, and the enemy replied with perhaps half as many. Some shells badly aimed wounded a few of our infantry (2 of my men), and I know killed and wounded hundreds, if not thousands, of the enemy. That night we were withdrawn to our original line of battle, after Lee found he could not dislodge the enemy. Pickett made several brilliant charges, but failed in driving the enemy from their walls. During the 4th everything was comparatively quiet except a cavalry fight on our right, which kept McLaws' Division under arms in line of battle all day. About 3 P.M. it closed, and then the gentle rain which had been falling just poured down all the evening. About 10 P.M. we got orders to march and in the rain by daylight had only gone 5 miles. All day Sunday, the 5th, we were standing about in the rain and mud, getting our wagons in line of march, and sending the wounded back to Williamsport and the prisoners on to the same point. The enemy at the same time fell back but where to, I have no idea. We came by way of Fairfield and on directly to Hagerstown. The enemy made several attempts to capture our wagon train, and did destroy a few, but paid dearly for it. We invariably whipped them off, or captured some of their men. We all arrived hereabouts on Tuesday and have been here since. What we are to do next, no one but Genl. Lee can tell. I learn he says he intends to fight them again north of the Potomac. I don't know, and hope not, for I think a fair calculation will stretch his loss since he crossed the Potomac on the 26th to about 18,000 or 20,000 men. The enemy's loss must be vastly larger, for we captured 11,000 prisoners. The Potomac is swimming and I imagine we will remain here till it falls, and then cross again into Virg., but cannot tell. I am sick of Maryland, and never want to come this side of the river again. As a Yankee prisoner told one of my men, we have found a great difference between invading the North and defending the South. . . .

Now, my darling, during all this campaign, I know you think I must have suffered. Well, of course I did more or less, but so much better than I expected did I stand it that I have no cause of complaining. During the three days' fighting I never felt better, and I suppose it was from mental excitement. I am as well as I could wish to be, and all this time have only prayed that I might be spared, not on my own account, but on yours, for I live only to make you happy, and life is doubly dear to me because I know we are happy when together, and because I believe I've got the sweetest family in the Confederacy. I pray God constantly that I may be spared to return safely to my dear family. We have no news from beyond the Potomac later than your letter of the 22nd June, which reached me last night. I trust you are all well yet. If we move into Virg. I'll write you as soon as possible afterwards, but if we do not, I don't know when I can write you again. I'll write as soon as I can at any rate, if I am spared. If I should be taken off in the next battle, I can only say I hope to meet you and mine in Heaven. Kiss our dear little pets for me. Give love to all the connections at home, and take for yourself my whole heart. . . . Goodbye, my dearest pet.

YOUR DEVOTED HUSBAND

— ★ —

Henry Owen served as a captain with Company C, 18th Virginia Volunteer Infantry.

———

Bunker Hill
Berkely Co., Va.
July 18th, 1863

MY DEAR HARRIET:

After the great battle of Gettysburg, our division had charge of a large lot of prisoners, some two hundred officers and thirty-three hundred privates. We guarded them from Gettysburg to Winchester, and had charge of them eight days. Our provisions were scarce.

The yankees had no utensils to cook with, and had to cook up the little flour that was issued to them in their tin cups and cook their small rations of beef on the coals. The officers were fine looking men in neat uniforms and were more intelligent than any lot of prisoners I have seen before at all. They parted with their canteens, knives, gold pencils, combs and many little trinkets to our soldiers for bread or meat, and I was sorry to see a disposition with our men to take all the advantage possible of the poor prisoners.

One day while at Williamsport, on this side of the Potomac, I went along the line of sentinels to see if all was safe. As I went strolling by a crowd, I found a young, fine looking officer trying to trade off a neat little pocket flask, silver mounted, for a half cake of bread. Our soldiers were trying to see how small a piece he would agree to take. I told this officer that he would soon have beef and flour issued to him and advised him to wait awhile, but he said he had never cooked any and did not know how to fix up his flour and beef. He said he was very hungry and wanted a piece of bread.

Some officers standing by were trying to dispute with him about the war, but he told them that he was a prisoner and it was unfair to ask him to argue the matter since if he spoke his sentiments freely they would be offended and that any arguments they might have would not affect the war at all nor end the strife a day sooner. They persisted, but he kept his eye and mind fixed upon the bread. I tried to get him off from the party. I had not gotten my rations that day and it was nine o'clock. I told him, however, that as soon as they came I would divide with him.

Soon afterwards, one of my men told me that he knew a house not far off where I could get breakfast. I went and got the yankee officer and told him if he would promise not to try to escape I would take him out to breakfast. He readily promised, and away we went over hill and dale together without even a pistol, chattering gaily as we promenaded together. We reached the house and got a splendid breakfast. The old lady and their daughters saw my old gray uniform and the yankee's dark blue cloth and they stirred about like the house was on fire. We were both very hungry and ate heartily of the old lady's light bread, fried ham, coffee (genuine) and honey.

When we got through, the old lady did not want to take my Confederate money. The yankee pulled out a full purse of his green backs and paid her for both of us. He then purchased three dozen biscuits and we jogged along back to camp. He was very thankful for my kindness and wanted me to accept his flask as a present, but I told him I did not charge for favors and that I had only done my duty to my fellow man in distress. He said I had fulfilled the scriptures, in that when I found mine enemy a-hungered I fed him. I told him that was my religion.

His flask was the neatest one I ever saw—silver mounted and covered with bamboo and whalebone, with a nice cord. It was all he had to carry water in, and I did not think it right to accept it. I told him all I wanted of his people was to be let alone, and unless they stopped the war we would fight them for a thousand years.

Before we parted, several for whom I done little favors came around and bid me goodbye and promised that if any of our regt. or my company ever fell into their hands they should be kindly attended to. When they left for Richmond, they all regretted to part with our brigade. One or two came forward and for the others thanked the brigade for their kindness and courtesy while with them and said they had found the bravest soldiers were the kindest to prisoners. . . .

I am the only Capt. left in our regt. and find a good deal of trouble in managing the men. I almost feel like deserting myself, and if I was to do so, don't you think you would kiss me and say it was all right?

I don't think we shall be called on soon to fight as we have been so cut up. My trust is in God for safety.

Yours faithfully as ever,
HENRY

— ★ —

William Nugent* served as a captain with the 28th Mississippi Cavalry. His letter was written after the fall of Vicksburg.

Camp near Brandon, Miss.
July 28th, 1863

MY OWN DEAR WIFE,

Corporal Robb of my Company has been furloughed, as well as several men from the Bolivar Company, and I take advantage of the opportunity to write you a letter, which I hope may serve to relieve you, in some measure, of the great anxiety that is superinduced by the present condition of our public affairs. Recently after the fall of V.Burg I entertained the most gloomy forbodings of the future; and indeed the great demoralization produced in our army thereby, added to the submissive spirit of the people generally, was enough to make one dispirited. The enemy have, however, ceased pursuing Johnston and have withdrawn their army to the hills of Warren to recruit. This will afford us an opportunity to reorganize and rediscipline our army and to call out our reserve: thus bringing us somewhat upon an equality with General Grant, whom, I hope, we may hereafter successfully encounter. If I am not greatly mistaken the possession of the River will prove a conquest barren of results. The West will soon discover that the trade upon which they heretofore throve has been ruined and that there are few or no customers for their redundant supplies. The fertile valley of the Mississippi has been desolated and the millions of dollars once realized by Western men thru the trade along the banks of our mighty River will be entirely lost. Our people have no money and no exchangeable commodity, and must be the recipients alone of bounties if they consume Western produce. The consequence of this state of things will, I hope, produce a state of indifference to the further prosecution of the war. We are now driven to fight to the bitter end, if conquest itself be the result. The ruling ma-

---

**Other letters by William Nugent appear on pages 56 and 175.

jority are contending to emancipate our slaves, and if the negroes are freed the country, as a general thing, is not worth fighting for at all. We will all be compelled to abandon it and seek some more congenial climate. Pemberton's Corps will be reorganized and placed under command of some more efficient General, who may succeed in bringing a little order out of a great deal of chaos. This being accomplished, we will have a pretty big army out here, which will be hard to whip. I have no idea we will attempt to hold the state west of the Mobile and Ohio R.Road, and believe our efforts will be directed to Genl. Rosecrans' Army first. In fact, we ought to be going there now as fast as possible. Our force added to Bragg's would enable [us] to whip the Army of the Cumberland, and this would accomplish more for our cause than the retention of Mobile. Jeff. Davis, tho', I fear will continue his old policy of endeavoring to hold fortified places and seabord cities to the great detriment of our cause. We need *concentration.* Charleston ought to have been left to take care of itself and Beauregard should have been sent to Lee's assistance. Johnston ought to have sent all possible reinforcements to Bragg and beat the life out of him while Grant was driving away at V.Burg; why it is our Generals can't see through a campaign I cannot discover. Their penetration does not extend below the surface and they are moving about utterly unconscious of the great issues now pending or of the magnitude of the task imposed upon us.

We are now lying here roasting in the sun, eating roasting ears and vegetables in the main. A little beef, an occasional leg of mutton and a boiled ham now and then constitute our bill of fare. Still we enjoy ourselves very well, and think our time is passing away pleasantly enough. We are daily in anticipation of orders to move—where no one knows unless it be Gen. Joe's confidants, who are few in number. Like our brethren of African descent we doze away the hours of noon under the shade of the broad oaks around us on a blanket, utterly oblivious of the morrow. We are fast becoming soldiers indeed. The other night I slept in the open air during a considerable rain and awoke in the morning very much refreshed. The rain didn't even give me a cold. Ben Johnston, Fowler and Capt. Blackburn are all absent sick and I cannot get a furlough. As soon as two of them return I will make my application, and try to get to you: I would risk capture to be allowed the privilege of remaining with you a few days. They are now giving two-week furloughs allowing travelling time in going to and returning from home. I had an amusing time with the boys drawing lots for furloughs. John and Tom Dunn *drew blanks* much to my regret. They have both become good soldiers, and by the steady attention to duty are entitled to some favor of the sort. The policy of giving furloughs should have been kept up from the beginning. It would have saved a great many of our men to us and prevented them from running off to see their families and make the necessary provision for them.

From the policy pursued by Genl. Sherman around V.Burg I judge you will not be in any danger at home. They will compel *you* to [give] him your slaves, perhaps, but will compel *them* to obey and respect you. You will be enabled to live, I hope. I gave Alf 50$ in La. money with which you can purchase the necessaries of life along the river, and will endeavor to procure more current money for you. As long as you are quiet and the country is not invaded by either army you can get along well; and being now within the lines and power of the enemy you will have to be politic.

My health continues to be tolerably fair—and promises to continue good during the balance of the summer. Our men are generally healthy, tho' we have a good many cases of intermittent fever, which readily yields to treatment. . . .

Good fortune and a kind Providence have attended me thus far and I hope this war will soon end and permit our reunion once more. Love and Kisses to all; and May God Almighty bless, comfort, direct and preserve you is the prayer of your

Ever devoted husband,
WILL

— ★ —

Spencer Glasgow Welch* served as a surgeon with the 13th South Carolina Volunteer Infantry.

Camp near Orange Court House, Virginia
August 2, 1863

DEAREST:

In a recent letter I promised to write you more about our campaign in Pennsylvania.

On the night of the 29th of June, we camped on the west side of the Blue Ridge Mountains, where they extend into Pennsylvania. On the morning of the next day (30th), we renewed our march. Shortly after starting, it began raining, but the road was hard and well macadamized and the rain made the march rather agreeable than otherwise.

On this same morning, we passed where a splendid iron factory had been burned by General Early, of Ewell's Corps. It belonged to a very celebrated lawyer and politician of Pennsylvania by the name of Thaddeus Stevens, who is noted for his extreme abolition[ist] views and his intense hatred for slave-holders. The works are said to have been worth more than one hundred thousand dollars. The burning had thrown a great many operatives out of employment, and they seemed to be much distressed.

During the day we wended our way up the mountains. The scene around us was very different from what we had just passed through. Instead of the enticing field and lovely landscape, we had now around us that which was rugged, grand and towering. In the afternoon about one or two o'clock we halted and bivouacked among the mountains. Our stopping-place was in a basin of the mountains which was very fertile and contained a few very excellent and highly cultivated farms. A while after we stopped, I started off to one of these farmhouses for the purpose of getting my dinner, as I was quite hungry and wanted something different from what I had been accustomed. . . .

---

*Another letter by Spencer Glasgow Welch appears on page 76.

DR. SPENCER GLASGOW WELCH

Upon returning to camp, I found that an order had been received during my absence to cook one day's rations and have it in haversacks and be ready to march at five o'clock next morning. This at once aroused our suspicions, for we concluded that we were about to meet the enemy. Next morning about five o'clock we began moving. We had not gone more than a mile and a half before our suspicions of the evening previous were fully verified and our expectations realized by the booming of cannon ahead of us in the direction of Gettysburg. Upon looking around, I at once noticed in the countenance of all an expression of intense seriousness and solemnity, which I have always perceived in the faces of men who are about to face death and the awful shock of battle.

As we advanced, the cannonading increased in fury. It was Heth's Division, ahead of ours, fighting. At last we arrived upon a hill where, upon another hill in front of us and about a half mile distant, we could see Heth's cannon arranged and booming away at Yankees, who were replying with considerable briskness, and we could also see the infantry of Heth's Division advancing in line of battle.

It was really a magnificent sight. The country was almost destitute of forest and was so open that it was easy to see all that was going on. Our division (Pender's) continued to keep within about half a mile of Heth's. McGowan's Brigade was at the right of the division and the 13th Regiment was at the right of the brigade. This being the case, I could see from one end of the division to the other as it moved forward in line of battle. It was nearly a mile in length.

The scene was certainly grand, taking all the surroundings into consideration. After Heth had driven the enemy some distance, it became necessary for our division to go to his support. McGowan's South Carolina and Scales' North Carolina Brigades were the first to relieve Heth. The hardest fighting did not begin until McGowan's and Scales' Divisions went into it. Then such a rattle of musketry I never heard surpassed. It lasted for about two hours and a half without cessation; and how many brave fellows went down in death in this short period of time!

Officers who have been in all the fights tell me that they never saw our brigade act so gallantly before. When the order was given to charge upon the enemy, who were lying behind stone fences and other places of concealment, our men rushed forward with a perfect fury, yelling and driving them, though with great slaughter to themselves as well as to the Yankees. Most of the casualties of our brigade occurred this day (July 1). As the enemy were concealed, they killed a great many of our men before we could get at them.

There were a good many dwellings in our path, to which the Yankees would also resort for protection, and they would shoot from the doors and windows. As soon as our troops would drive them out, they would rush in, turn out the families and set the houses on fire. I think this was wrong, because the families could not prevent the Yankees seeking shelter in their houses. I saw some of the poor women who had been thus treated. They were greatly distressed, and it excited my sympathy very much. These people would have left their houses, but the battle came on so unexpectedly to them, as is often the case, that they had not time. . . .

The fighting on the first day ceased about night, and when our brigade was relieved by Lane's North Carolina Brigade, it was nearly dark. I returned to the hospital, and on my way back came to Anderson's Division of our corps (Hill's) lying in line of battle at least two miles to the rear of where the advance column was. Pender's Division and Heth's had been fighting all day, and they were exhausted, besides being terribly "cut up."

When they drove the Yankees to the long high range of hills, which the Yankees held throughout the fight, they should have been immediately reinforced by Anderson with his fresh troops. Then the strong position last occupied by the enemy could have been taken, and the next day, when Ewell and Longstreet came up, the victory completely won. If "Old Stonewall" had been alive and there, it no doubt would have been done. Hill was a good division commander, but he is not a superior corps commander. He lacks the mind and sagacity of Jackson. . . .

On the second day of the battle, the fighting did not begin until about twelve or one o'clock, from which time until night it raged with great fury. The reason it began so late in the day was because it required some time for Ewell and Longstreet to get their forces in position.

On the third day, the fighting began early in the morning and continued with the greatest imaginable fury all day; at one time, about three o'clock in the afternoon, with such a cannonading I never heard before. About 150 pieces of cannon on our side and as many or more on the side of the enemy kept up for several hours. It was truly terrifying and was like heavy skirmishing in the rapidity with which the volleys succeeded one another. The roar of the artillery, the rattle of the musketry and the wild terrific scream of the shells as they whizzed through the air was really the most appalling situation that could possibly be produced. Our troops (Pickett's Division) charged the enemy's strong position, which they had now entrenched, but with no avail, although we slaughtered thousands of them.

On the night of the 3rd, General Lee withdrew the army nearly to its original position, hoping, I suppose, that the enemy would attack him; but they didn't come out of their strongholds, for well they knew what their fate would be if they met the Confederate Army of Virginia upon equal grounds. On the 4th, our army remained in line of battle, earnestly desiring the advance of the Yankees, but they did not come. During this day the rain fell in torrents, completely drenching the troops.

A while after dark, we began to leave, but took a different and nearer route to the Potomac than the one we had just passed over. Though nearer, it was very rough and not macadamized, and the passing of wagons and artillery over it cut it up horribly and made it almost impassable. Yet over this road our large army had to pass. I was lucky enough to get into a medical wagon and rode until next morning. It rained nearly all night, and such a sight as our troops were next day! They were all wet and many of them muddy all over from having fallen down during the night.

On July 5, we recrossed the Blue Ridge Mountains. Climbing the mountains was very tedious after so much toil, excitement and loss of sleep, but we met with no obstacle until we came to Hagerstown, Md., where we stopped on account of the Potomac's being too high to ford. While [we were] here, the Yankees came up. Our army was placed in line to meet them, but they did not dare to attack. In this situation we remained for several days with them in sight of us.

After a pontoon bridge was finished at Falling Waters and the river was sufficiently down to ford at Williamsport, we left the vicinity of Hagerstown. It was just after dark when we began leaving. It was a desperately dark night and such a rain I thought I never before knew to fall. I did not meet with such luck as the night we left Gettysburg, Pa., but had to walk all night, and such a road I think troops never before traveled over. It appeared to me that at least half of the road was a quagmire, coming in places nearly to the knees.

Hill's Corps went by Falling Waters and Longstreet's and Ewell's by Williamsport, where they had to wade the river, which was still very deep, coming up nearly to the shoulders. The pontoon bridge was at Falling Waters, where we crossed. Our division was in the rear at this place, and when we got within about a mile and a half of the river we halted to enable the wagons ahead to get out of the way.

Being very tired, we all lay down and nearly everyone fell asleep. Suddenly the Yankee cavalry rushed upon us, firing and yelling at a furious rate. None of our guns were loaded and they were also in a bad fix from the wet of the previous night. They attacked General Pettigrew's North Carolina Brigade first. Our brigade was lying down fifty yards behind his. I was lying down between the two brigades near a spring. General Pettigrew was killed here. I was close to him when he was killed. It was a serious loss to the service. We fought them for some time. Then General Hill sent an order to fall back across the river, and it was done in good order.

The attack was a complete surprise, and is disgraceful either to General Hill or General Heth. One is certainly to blame. The Yankees threw shells at the bridge and came very near hitting it just as I was about to cross; but, after we were close enough to the river not to be hurt by our own shells, our cannon on this side opened upon them, which soon made them "skedaddle" away.

— ★ —

William Nugent* served as a captain with the 28th Mississippi Cavalry.

———

Hd. Qrs. Cavalry Brigade
Tupelo, Miss., Sept. 7th, 1863

MY DARLING WIFE,

The hour of your trial is approaching and I feel very very uneasy on your account. I hope and trust in the Giver of all good, though the thought that you are so far away, so near the enemy's lines and surrounded by so many dangers makes me feel quite blue at times: and were it not for the elasticity of mind and heart which characterizes me, I should have long since grown utterly despondent.

War is fast becoming the thing natural, tho' abhorrent to my feelings. I go at it just as I used to go at law-suits. Still I am not by any manner of means fond of the profession. The idea of being continually employed in the destruction of human life is revolting in the extreme. Necessity, imperious and exacting, forces us along and we hurry through the dreadful task apparently unconscious of its demoralizing influences and destructive effects both upon the nation and individuals. I wish *Uncl. Saml.* would recognize his nephew and give us peace. I do not desire a reconstruction and a hollow truce, a servile place in the family of nations and to eat the bread of dependence while I am denied all the privileges of a freeman. The Yankees say that when we are conquered they cannot afford to let us have the right of trial by jury, because they say a "secesh" jury would clear us all, neither can we have our own judges or exercise the elective franchise. This is the doctrine held

———

*Other letters by William Nugent appear on pages 56 and 166.

by their main supporters and is the one which will be practiced by them if they are successful. And yet our weak-minded friends are willing to lick the hand that would smite them and pay court to the hardhearted minions of abolitionism. I own no slaves and can freely express my notions without being taxed with any motive of self interest. I know that this country without slave labor would be wholly worthless, a barren waste and desolate plain—we can only live and exist by this species of labor: and hence I am willing to continue the fight to the last. If we have to succumb we must do it bravely fighting for our rights; and the remnant must migrate. If the worst comes, we must go over to England or France, and become Colonies again. Never will I be content to submit to Yankee rule. The Russian yoke would be preferable. The close fisted Yankees would filch our pockets at every turn— France I would prefer. Her policy is more enlightened than that of England and she would give us the rights and privileges of freemen. It would be her policy and doubtless when her affairs are straightened in Mexico, she will recognize the importance of a more decided policy in American affairs.

I hope the enemy now discovers that the possession of the River is a barren victory. Their Western produce finds no market and the foreign demand will not be very large or extensive either at New Orleans. Their commerce is fettered by childish restrictions and the Southern *privateers* keep them uneasy. Cotton cannot be found and *flour and bacon* is not a commodity of much exchangeable value. A few men, *in authority,* may make fortunes; but the poor man who brings his flat load of corn and potatoes expecting to return with a pocket full of money will be utterly mistaken. The Yankees won't see this until too late to remedy the evil. They are not far-seeing enough. If they only had the negroes at work on the plantations under their masters, they would have realized some beneficial results.

We are now camped at a place memorable in this war, and whose name will live in history. We are occupying Genl. Bragg's old Hd. Qrs. and have a cozy time of it—and if the enemy don't disturb us soon we will be quite comfortably fixed. . . .

Old Pillow is conscripting every man in the whole country. He is no respecter of persons. There is in consequence a terrific quaking among the noncombatants and substitute men. Judge Handy has just decided that the principal is liable unless his substitute is over 45 yrs. of age; and is in any event liable for *militia duty.* This will make the nice young gentlemen quake in their shoes, and force them to "come to the centre."

My health continues good—I am endeavoring to get Clarence promoted so that he can come up here and be with me, and, I think I will succeed in due course of time. The Company is, I am sorry to have to say, going to pieces, numbering now only some twenty-nine men for duty.

Give my love and kisses to all. Do the best you can, and ever remember that you are supreme in my affections. May God Almighty bless, comfort, protect and preserve you is the prayer of

Your devoted husband,

WILL

— ★ —

Henry Curtis served as a lieutenant with the 37th Illinois Volunteer Infantry. He was also staff officer to Brigadier General Julius White. Lieutenant Curtis wrote this letter during the Siege of Knoxville.

Knoxville, Tennessee
November 21, 1863

Being a rainy day and nothing doing, I will write you, though when this will get through is very problematical. On the night of the 13th, we got word that the enemy were building a pontoon bridge six miles below us. I took twenty-five cavalry and made for it, leaving orders for a regiment section of artillery to follow.

It was very dark and there was but one road down the point, at the extremity of which the bridge was and the woods each side were impassable with undergrowth. I expected a vigorous opposition and never hated a job worse in my life. However, by scientific

LIEUTENANT HENRY CURTIS

maneuvering, I got to within 250 yards of the bridge and to within 50 yards of a heavy picket without firing.

Sent for the infantry to come out, but they had been ordered back—could get no further than I was, as the road was a narrow lane. I waited until near daylight and fell back. Reported I could get no more men. I went down again with 30 men, about halfway, the rebels being advanced. Took a position in an old church and held it with some occasional firing. [Brigadier General Julius] White wanted me to go on, but I sent him word that I could not without more men. Burnside had now got to our position (where the brigade was). I had sent a small regiment of cavalry to my aid. They were scared and stayed some four miles back. Burnside sent me orders to go on. Of course I went with what I had, though I had told White and him a dozen times I could do nothing but should get whipped and surrounded. Charged up a big hill in front, got the fire of about 200 men and got well whipped in a very few moments. Drew back and had just formed a line when about 100 rebels opened on my rear from the only road to get off by. They were right on us, and the chance looked bad. Only one side was open and they were making for that. Away we went over fences and through brush on the full run and bullets flying thick enough. Got out at last, losing three killed, some half dozen wounded and as many horses. Lost about six prisoners, their horses being shot and they caught.

White was coming up with the brigade, but I did not know it, I could only get back by circling round some fifteen miles at Lenoir [City], a town six miles from our camp.

Camped for the night, it being dark, and the next morning went after the brigade. Burnside had gone on the evening before with the 9th A.C. and our brigade and driven the rebels nearly to the bridgehead. I found them on the retreat again, it not appearing advisable for him to go on. We lost some 100 men or more driving them in. Hope B. got it satisfactorily into his head, that twenty cavalry couldn't go to the bridge!

The bridge is precisely where I told the chief of engineers it would be, but he, being a West Point man, of course would not admit I would know anything! We fell back to Lenoir [City] that night, and I went into line. Only one small brush in the night and we killed a couple of rebels. . . .

Our brigade (one being away) took the advance at 3:00 A.M. At 12:00 P.M., we went into line at Campbell's Station, fifteen miles from Knoxville. The 9th A.C. was now fighting heavily. We were to let it pass and check the rebels. They came down thick, but we broke from lines and held them until dark. Fell back a mile, our brigade holding the enemy and coming off splendidly. General B. said he never saw troops behave so well on a field of battle.

At dark, started for this place, our brigade in rear, arrived next morning and are now in position and fortifying. Got no hits myself. One shell hit right beside my horse and two shrapnel burst right in my face but never a scratch did I get. We're now on the defensive here—enemy are very slow and I think can't take us in; if they do you'll not see this. We fire occasionally and so do they. We have enough food for present purposes and are in good health.

Was pretty well worn out when I got here, having no sleep, nothing to eat, and being in the saddle day and night from the start some twenty-four hours longer than most of the others. Am now quite recuperated. November 29th—still besieged. The rebels made assaults early this morning but were repulsed. We took some 300 prisoners. December 4th, reinforcements arrived at last.

— ★ —

Frank Phelps served as a sergeant with the 10th Wisconsin Volunteer Infantry. The following letter was written after the Chattanooga, Tennessee, Campaign.

————

Camp at Chattanooga, Tenn.
Dec. 2, 1863

MY DEAR FRIENDS,
Again has the army of the Cumberland with Hooker's and Grant's brave boys routed and scattered Bragg's Army while yet

exulting over their dear bought victory, if you call it that, of Chickamauga. You have ere this seen detailed accounts of the fight, but yet it may be interesting to know what I saw and did in the fight though the latter part was very small.

I will commence away back to the first signs we got of an advance movement. On the 19th of last month we had orders for each man to have 100 rounds of ammunition. The usual amount we have to carry is only 40 rounds, so we knew something was up. The next day, we had orders to go on picket with two days' rations. Well, we went out, when it commenced to rain and rained almost every hour we were out.

While we were on the lines, we were not very far apart, only a little creek between us. The rebs were very friendly, coming down on the bank to trade papers, canteens or anything they could get. I had a *New York Tribune,* which I exchanged for an Augusta paper. The next day I exchanged a Wis. *State Journal* for the *Richmond News.* They wanted to get playing cards the most. One fellow offered me Greenbacks or gold if I would get him some. He said they had to pay $12 per pack for them and they were good for nothing.

We were on two days, and at the station where we were, 27 rebels deserted and came over. We were relieved on the morning of the 22nd. That afternoon we received orders to be ready to move at 6 A.M. on the 23rd. We got ready and then the order was countermanded. We were not to leave camp, but to hold ourselves ready to move at a moment's notice. At noon, we were ordered to move out into the rifle pits. The position of our brigade and division is on the extreme right, and we expected that we were going to make for Lookout Mountain, or that there would be a general advance. At one o'clock, our heavy guns from Fort Wood and all along the lines opened on the enemy.

Soon we heard skirmishing on the left. Then we understood the movement. After some heavy firing, our forces drove the rebels from their rifle pits. When we stopped for the night, we were not allowed to leave the works as the rebels might make a movement on our right. During the night, we were moved up to support a battery of 20-pound Parrotts. Just before daylight, we were ordered to leave half of the regiment there (which was only 30 men) and take the rest down to Louis battery. The rest of the brigade had moved out to the front.

The next morning we expected to have a fight, but it was still all along the lines. At 10 o'clock, there was some firing away off in Lookout Valley where Hooker had his camps. Pretty soon the firing became more general and the first thing we saw was our men charging up Lookout Mountain. It commenced to rain about noon and it was so foggy we could not see very well. At dark, we held the mountain. Our brigade had driven the rebels on this side and joined Hooker. We expected to go out and join the brigade during the night, but they could get no horses for the battery, so we had to stay.

The next morning was clear, but awful cold. The rebs had left Lookout Mountain and our forces had gone over through the valley toward Missionary Ridge. Hooker had got to Rossville, which place we made our stand on Monday. Left here is a large gap or pass between the two ridges. From this place Hooker could come up in the rear of the rebels on Mission[ary] Ridge. Sherman with Grant's *Western boys* had gone up the river to where Chickamauga Creek empties into the river and crossed over, bagging about 100 rebs that were making rafts to float down the river to break our pontoon bridges. Here we took possession of a large knob on the north end of Mission[ary] Ridge, while Maj. Gen. Howard with the 11th Corps opened communications with Sherman from this way. . . .

Soon I could see our line advance. Our brigade held the right, forward they went, but the hill was steep and high and the rebels were packed in their rifle pits. Our men come up within range when they fire and charge up with the bayonet. The rebels either retreat or surrender. After charging the rebels out of five lines of rifle pits, we reach the top of the hill and, almost at the same time, the batteries of the rebels stop firing. They have been firing on Sherman and Thomas as fast as guns could be worked. A cheer reaches us, and on the the double quick do our men face towards Sherman and go to his relief.

The rebel center is broken. We have got all of their heavy guns and hold possession of all the ridge except where the railroad goes through. There the rebels have massed the remainder of their army. From that point they can rake the whole ridge with grape and canister. We can see 20 different guns open almost at the same instant. Guns that had been firing towards Sherman all the forenoon are now firing in the opposite direction. The roar of musketry and artillery is heavier than before; a huge column of smoke rises away over to our right. The rebels are burning their stores. Hooker is working there. Night comes on and the rebels hold their position on Tunnel Hill. Sherman had been repulsed three times, but the fourth time he was victorious and the rebels had to leave.

That night, all was still. Bragg's Army had been defeated and driven from every position. *Chickamauga had been avenged.* That night our forces bivouacked in the rebel camp. The next morning our forces were in pursuit of the retreating rebels. At Ringold, Bragg tried to make another stand. He had chosen a good position, but our column, which went on our old road from Bridgeport, over the mountain to Trenton, came up in his rear, and joined onto Hooker. He was soon driven from there. Here our army had to stop on account of supplies. During the night our brigade started back and reached here the next afternoon. Bragg lost all of his artillery and about 15,000 prisoners. This is the first fight down in this section of the country that the old 10th was not in the front ranks. Our brigade was there and we would have been if we had officers, but one regiment had to be left back, and we were the lucky regiment. . . .

Yours as ever,
FRANK W. PHELPS

— ★ —

Aden Cavins* served as a lieutenant colonel with the 97th Indiana Volunteer Infantry.

———————

Scottsboro, Ala.
Dec. 30, 1863

MY DEAR TILLA:

All your letters express dread of harm to me in the battles around Chattanooga. You no doubt before this time have heard that I am still a breathing, moving corporal being.

We left Stevenson at the time I wrote you. We arrived here on the Memphis and Charleston railroad, a distance of twenty-seven miles over the worst roads for a level country I ever saw.

The weather grew warmer soon after I wrote you and it rained almost incessantly for four days. Our wagons only arrived here last evening, nearly worn out. We have our tents put up now and have dried ourselves and feel quite comfortable. It is expected that we will remain here for two weeks and then move farther along the road so as to be able to get forage for our teams. . . .

A majority of the southern people whose homes are now within the federal lines are sick of the war and want peace on any terms. Texas and Louisiana have already deserted their confederates and their soldiers have made their way to their homes. Thousands of others are only waiting an opportunity to do the same thing. Northern Alabama is full of deserters from the rebel army. It is said that there are at least five hundred in this country. But when you get a man from south of our lines, he speaks as hopefully as Jeff Davis, and says that they would rather die than have any left to witness their subjugation.

I, a few months ago, spoke to those who are now leaving them at every opportunity. But when they were shut out from their homes, their friends, and the dear ones that aforetime smiled happily around their firesides, they were subdued—not by federal bayonets or the fierce rattle of our dreadful musketry, but by

*Other letters by Aden Cavins appear on pages 42 and 204.

sentiments deeply established in the constitution of man: love of home, wife, father, mother or children. There is a point beyond which few can go. One may endure any physical hardship, to gratify a feeling, a prejudice or a whim, or suffer death rather than a real or supposed dishonor. But most men are subdued when the ties of early life are sundered and all the joyous memories of "home, sweet home" are trampled under foot.

When, therefore, the rebels are driven from their homes and their places become occupied by our soldiers; when they are separated from their families by long and tedious days, they will give up the contest. However, they are now driven into so few of their pretended states that want may soon begin to wear on them. But misguided people will never consult their best interests until disasters, dreadful and ruinous, will overtake them.

I believe during the next summer and fall campaign most of their country will be overrun, and after that nothing but lawless bands of guerrillas will prevent the soldiers from returning home. Texas will be mostly conquered this winter; Arkansas, Louisiana and Mississippi are almost subjugated; their once fair fields are nothing but wastes—fences and barns and houses destroyed and all their substance and stock destroyed. Alabama and Georgia will have to yield in the next movement.

The rebels have a large army and will have months to recruit it and gather up their scattered forces. What jealousies and discords may happen among them no one can guess, but unless something supervenes to thwart the intentions of the rebel leaders, there will be at least one more year of fierce savage war, and then I think the struggle will be over. I hope that dissensions, brawls and discord may creep into their ranks, so as to hurry up the time when all can join those they love so well and whose absence they so much regret. It will most truly be a day of rejoicing when the war-worn soldier returns to the side of his dear ones, where he can view them affectionately by day and rest sweetly with them by night.

I am glad Charley is reading *Plutarch's Lives*. There is so much of the noble, generous and heroic acts in the narratives that it cannot fail making a lasting impression on his mind. You must see that he pronounces the proper names correctly. See Classical Dictionary.

My love to all. Write often.

— ★ —

Frederick Bartleson served as a colonel with the 100th Illinois Volunteer Infantry. Colonel Bartleson's letter to his wife was written while he was in Confederate captivity at Libby Prison.

February 26, 1864

DEAR KATE:

I take this opportunity of sending you a longer letter than usual by the hands of a prisoner who has been exchanged. Owing to the fact that many here do nothing else but write letters, which, of course, as one would expect, are to be read, such an accumulation of letters ensued that an order has been issued, unduly severe, prohibiting more than one letter a week, and that to contain no more than six lines. This will account for what you have doubtless regarded as very brief epistles. . . .

The question of exchange looks black, but perhaps it may clear up one of these days. Some special exchanges are being affected, and it is said that Capts. Sawyer and Flum, who were once on a line selected to be hanged, are to be exchanged.

You noticed the arrival of a number of officers who had escaped from Libby by means of a tunnel. It was, I think, the most clever performance in that line during the war, and we could see them coming up from their subterranean hole and issuing on the street in full view of the guards. Of course, there was great rivalry as to who should go, as all could not. For my part, I could only look on with regret, as it was impossible for me to crawl through or to make the descent, which was through a fireplace to the ground floor, where the tunnel was commenced. Some have been brought back, but the rest are safe. But the difficulties after getting out are very formidable. The country is swarming with scouts and patrols on the lookout for deserters. . . .

Considering our number in this prison, it is a matter of as much congratulation as wonder that we are so healthy here. The same cannot be said of the Island. But there is very little smallpox among us, while it is said to be quite bad elsewhere. I was vaccinated and it took slightly.

My daily life: I go to bed about ten, get up a little after daylight for roll-call, then breakfast. Read, write, walk and talk and grumble for a while. At two P.M., roll-call, then have dinner. Read, write, talk and grumble till bedtime. Not a great variety, to be sure. . . .

Being confined in a building, with insufficient exercise, is very irksome. But there is nothing which does not become systematic, and Libby has its life and its routine and its characters. I wish Dickens could paint and describe it. When I first came here, there was a newspaper edited by a chaplain and published weekly. It contained some good articles occasionally. Then for a long time there were French classes and German classes, and some soldiers improved the time very well.

Now, in regard to the relative treatment of prisoners by respective Governments, I have a word to say. No man can say that prisoners are as well treated there as they are here. There are two reasons against it; one is, they haven't got the means to treat them as well, and another is, they haven't got the disposition. They are fighting from different motives from us. We are fighting for the Union, a sentiment, a high and noble sentiment, but after all a sentiment. They are fighting for independence and are animated by passion and hatred against invaders.

When men fight for independence, it makes no difference whether the cause is just or not. You can get up an amount of enthusiasm that nothing else will excite. And while we feed our prisoners well, and it is our policy to do it, and while public sentiment would not justify any other course, they feed theirs they are not particular how. Public sentiment there will justify almost any treatment of the Yankees.

When a box is received, there is great joy with the recipient. If it is a dull season for boxes, great crowds gather around with the most vociferous cries and pass critically on each article received, tickled to death, like a child with a new toy. This prison life almost makes one a child again, and it is reason, undoubtedly, which purifies a man's mind and makes him think he will be better when he gets out. Render him liable to good impressions—you imagine how I get along here.

The whole secret of making it endurable consists in having something to do. When I am in good trim and my mind is clear, I manage to make the day pass tolerably. Something to do at stated hours, making one forget where he is, is the secret. When there was a general belief that an exchange would be affected, I broke in on my ordinary pursuits and devoted myself to tracing the reliability of the rumors, which flowed in on us like a flood. I was more dissatisfied at that time than almost any other, when our hope vanished; so little doubt had I entertained, previous to that time, of the success of the negotiations which were going on.

A rumor here on exchange is dissected and analyzed with the utmost skill and acuteness. A thousand minds, eager and watchful, are brought to bear upon it. And no matter how absurd it may appear at first, it is gravely considered from all angles. Your old maid is no match at all for the Libby gossips. Curiosity here beats the most inquisitive form of that article elsewhere—and as for the exaggerations of a rumor after it is once started, no one can imagine them. I do not believe that on this subject it is possible for any inmate here to tell the truth. I am accustomed to say that here it requires twelve men to tell the truth.

We are made up here, as you can well imagine, of every variety of character and disposition. Sometimes I am sorry to say that the temper of some few is overcome and that fight is the consequence. We have had one or two of these little affairs since I have been here, but they were stopped. Of course, there is a public sentiment which condemns all such things, but in a population numbering nine hundred, we constitute a little village without the restraints of home.

The vermin are troublesome, so please put something in the box to help keep them off. We have bed bugs, too, and I presume that in the summer, we will find them very bad. . . .

Now, dear Kate, I think this letter is long enough. I have not sent it through the mail in the ordinary way, but through the favor of a friend.

My love is all for you. Remember and give my love to all our friends.

Faithfully,
FRED

After his release from Libby Prison, Colonel Bartleson was killed at the Battle of Kenneshaw Mountain, Georgia, June 27, 1864.

— ★ —

At the time of writing, Henry Morrison* was serving as a captain with the 4th Virginia Volunteer Infantry. His letter was written on the opening day of the Battle of the Wilderness in Virginia.

May 5th, 1864
near Spotsylvania

MY DEAR AUNT:

I have an opportunity of sending a letter to the office, and as I have not written to you yet I will write a short note to apprise you of our safety thus far.

We have been on the march backward and forward in the wilderness for two days. On Wednesday, we were to have a grand review of our corps and were saddling our horses for that purpose when we ordered to pack up everything and move out immediately. In ten minutes, we were mounted and moving off at a fast gait. Late in the evening, we got in hearing of our sharpshooters, who were sent out from a regiment of our brigade.

---

*Another letter by Henry Morrison appears on page 213.

Yesterday I rode pretty hard all day. Ruff and myself were detached with eight or ten others from the regiment to go out toward the nearest picket. After staying there until the regiment had gotten many miles ahead, we had to overtake it. We did that just as it was starting off at a fast trot to meet the Yankees and relieve General Lomax, who, with his brigade, had been engaged all evening.

When we got into position, our squadron was dismounted and sent out as sharpshooters. We concealed ourselves in a thicket of pines and laid there from three or four miles to this place. We could see the Yankees very distinctly a short distance in front of us but they did not advance. They only fired into the bushes once or twice with artillery.

I think the fight has commenced in earnest now. At this moment, we can hear the artillery roaring on our right. Occasionally we hear a volley of musketry. The sun is just rising and how beautiful! It makes one feel sad to think this beautiful spring day

The camp of the 114th Pennsylvania Infantry, Brandy Station, Virginia, March 1864

must be spent just slaughtering human beings. This is likely to prove a memorable day in the history of our country.

Everything is unusually still in camp. Nothing disturbs the quiet except the singing of birds and the roar of arms. We're saddled up and will move on pretty soon, I expect. My mare is getting very low in [marching] order. I'm afraid this fight will put her past traveling.

Remember me affectionately to all at home, white and black. Write soon.

— ★ —

Chester Tuttle served as a private with Company I, 81st New York Volunteer Infantry. His letter was written after the Union victory at the Battle of the Wilderness.

Camp of 81st N.Y. Vols., Virginia
May 11th/64

DEAR BROTHER ELMUS:

I was just sitting down to write to you when your letter to Squire was received. Was glad to hear from you but sorry to hear of Franky's misfortune. Elmus, I have got a great deal to tell you if I only knew how to tell it.

The 4th of May the 18th Army corps (of which our brigade forms a part) & the 10th A.C. left Yorktown on transports; sailed down by Ft. Monroe and up the James river and landed 4 miles above City Point. From there we marched 7 miles, where we are now fortified. I cannot tell you exactly our position. It is between Petersburg & Richmond 8 miles from the former & 18 miles from the latter. There has been fighting nearly every day since we have been here. First the railroad had to be torn up, which the rebels strongly objected to, but while our batteries played on them one of our regiments made a charge on it and literally lifted the rails and ties out of their beds and lifted them over in the ditch.

PRIVATE CHESTER TUTTLE

The first three days after we came here our regiment did picket duty. The rebs did not come near us so all we had to do was to lay and listen to the firing, sleep, and eat. Sunday our regiment was relieved and we had orders to be ready for *work* the next day. We were waked up at three the next morning and after a hasty breakfast we were marched to the front towards Rigs and deployed as skirmishes and then came the *work*. We had to skirmish through the woods which the fire had run through the day before and it was like walking through an ash heap. I could hardly breathe, my nose and mouth was so full of dust and ashes. For about 4 miles we tramped till we came out on top of a hill that overlooked the railroad; *then we saw the rebs.* At the foot of the hill was a valley (cleared) through which ran the railroad and on the other side of that was another wooded hill. In the edge of those woods was a strong force of rebel cavalry and infantry, and when we appeared on the brow of the hill their bullets whistled around us pretty sharp. We halted in the woods but did not return their fire. The rebs drew back in their woods and there we were each waiting for the other. It would have been foolishness for us to charge on them with no line of skirmishes and no support.

Word was sent back for another brigade and scouts were sent out ahead to watch for any movement the enemy might make. I volunteered for a scout and went down the hill till I came to the cleared land, when I sat down under a tree and paid my attention to the opposite woods. Once in awhile a horseman would come out of the woods and after taking a look over our way go back again. Everything was quiet. There was a large white farm house across the railroad but no one was stirring around it. In a couple of hours our support came up and orders were given for the skirmish line to advance and if we were fired on . . . to hold our ground till our brigade could pass through our line and charge on them. We descended into the valley and over the railroad expecting every minute to hear their balls whistling round our heads, but the rebs had put out. . . . Our line was halted right by the house and I happened to be the nearest one to it and went up on the steps. . . . There was no one there but a couple of dogs that had more attachment for their home than fear of the Yankees and so had not followed their master.

The commander of the skirmishes came up on the steps and ordered me to break open the door. I kicked it open and we went in. Most of the hinges had been removed but there was still some valuable things left. Evidently the owner of the house was rich. There was a Spinet Piano in one of the rooms. I went into the dining room. There the table was spread with costly dishes, napkins to every plate. I would have taken a good many things if I could have carried them. Our line was again ordered forward and we again entered the woods. . . .

We had not gone far before we came across 2 rebels lying side of a tree. They were sick and had to fall out and be taken prisoners. Their regiment was not a great ways ahead of us. Keeping on, we came to a road that run through the woods. Looking down it, we saw a brass piece stationed in the weeds. We were in doubt at first which side it belonged to for it was so far off we could not tell how the men were dressed and we did not know but our artillery had got out as far as that, but soon our doubts were dispelled, for a puff of smoke issued from the gun and a shell came screeching down the road. You would have laughed could you have seen the men fall on their faces in the dirt and then shelter themselves in the woods. For about half an hour we lay there while the rebs sent their shells into the woods "right-smart." Every shell would burst right over our heads but no one was hurt. If the shells had burst before they reached us some one would have got hurt, but they were going with such force that the pieces were carried right on beyond us. After awhile they stopped and we moved on.

We had not gone ten rods before we walked into an ambuscade of rebs. The bullets flew around us then but there was not much damage done, the woods were so thick and the rebs were too impatient. They did not wait till we got where they could see the "whites of our eyes." One man got a ball through his leg (and it had to be taken off), another man more unlucky had one through his brains. Some whistled pretty darned close to me. I did not have a very big tree to get behind and my coat pockets was stuck full of southern papers and a white shirt I had taken out of the house, so I was a good mark for them. We did not fire a shot for we saw no one to fire at. They were so effectually concealed, and the bushes were so thick, that not even the smoke of their guns could be seen. We backed out of that for they were too "many *guns*" for us. Our company backed out so quick they left three men and myself in there all alone. We were watching so close for a rebel that we did not see that the company had left till we heard the order given to form a new line. We got back—formed a new line —a battery came up and shelled them and another regiment came and relieved us and our regiment was marched back to a creek to give us a little rest. (Our regiment was completely tired out. We had skirmished from 4 A.M. till 3 P.M. A great many had fallen down sun struck but we had not—still more than half an hour before we were again taken up to the front and formed in line of battle. The enemy continued shelling the woods and our battery returned the fire. At dark the firing ceased. The enemy lost near 300 men that day by our division. They charged on one of our batteries just as two regiments came up to support it when they in turn gave them a volley and charged them.

That night a strong picket was posted in front with our brigade for a support.

During the night they made two charges on our picket but was repulsed each time. Our boys laughed a good deal to hear the rebels yell when they charged. They sounded like old women trying to drive crows out of the garden. When *our* men charged it sounded like *men*. The rebs did a good thing for us when they attacked our pickets. When we lay down at night our shirts was wet as water with sweat and we did not have even a rubber blanket to cover us and every time they waked us up our bodies were cold as ice. After getting up and exercising a little we got warmer and prevented us from catching cold. We could hear the cars running all night on the other railroad fetching troops down from Richmond or sending them *to* Richmond (uncertain which). The next morning we were marched to some rifle pits, where we were kept all day, and at night we were marched back to Camp, where we arrived completely worn out. I don't know where the rebs went to that was in front of us or whether they were withdrawn or not.

I think they went to Petersburg (the main force) it was only 3 miles from there.

Elmus, I have told you all I know about *our* operations. You know that a soldier does not know much about what is done only as it comes under his own observation. We may be in the thickest part of a battle and not know how the thing was carried on until we read [about it]. You will probably read the account of our operations in the papers and will then know more about it than we do. Our army lays near the river so we are under the protection of the gun boats. It would not do for us to go out in the interior far because there is only two Corps of us and if the rebs got in between us and the river they would raise the devil with us. I suppose the most we are here for is to draw the attention of the enemy from Gen Meade. . . .

Gen Gillmore is here in Command of the 10th Corps, he is on our right, he had a fight with the enemy and made them retreat. They took some prisoners who told quite a laughable story about one of their Cols. He brought them down from Richmond and would practice them on charging all the way down so they would know how to do it when they met us. When they got down here the first one of our regiments they met was a Connecticut regiment with 7 shorters. He charged his regt on them and received a volley that killed some. He says "Charge again before they have time to load" but they received another volley. The Col thought surely that there could be no more guns loaded and *tried it again*. Our men let into them, killing the Col and a good part of his men. The rest were taken prisoners. They were surprised to find that our men had four more charges ready for them if needed.

Elmus, we have a few cowards in Comp I. When we first came in sight of the rebs and our skirmish line was ordered to advance on them, Martin says "I am sick" and he put back for the rear. Three or four more put back when the shells were thrown over our heads. These men will never hear the last of it as long as they are in the company.

It is very hot here, the woods are on fire all the time. Our men are out fighting it now to keep it from getting into our camp.

I don't hear any firing now. I guess both armies are resting. Squire is writing a letter home. The mail came in today. Squire got your letter and I got one from Mary. I did not expect we would get any till we got back. It seemed good to get a letter from home. I hope we will have some more fights and I will write you about them if I come out all right. But I will say goodbye now.

Give our love to all the folks.

FROM YOUR BROTHER CHESTER

PS That house that I went into was afterwards used for our wounded. The Piano was used to cut off legs and arms on. Ben Ballard was there helping take care of the wounded. He said that the blood run down in on to the strings.

Chester Tuttle was killed in action at the Second Battle of Cold Harbor, Virginia, on June 4, 1864.

— ★ —

Eugene Blackford* served as a major with the 5th Alabama Volunteer Infantry. His letter home was written during the Spotsylvania Courthouse Campaign, which lasted from May 7–19, 1864.

Hd. Qtrs. 5th Infantry
In line of battle
near Spotsylvania C.H., Va.
14th May, 1864

MY DEAR SISTER:

Tho the shells are bursting all around us and the minie bullets are cheeping just over our heads, we have dug ourselves deep enough into the ground to be tolerably protected and enough for me to write a few lines to tell you how delighted I was to hear that

*Another letter by Eugene Blackford appears on page 8.

you had finally taken the great step. I have never spoken with you upon this subject for obvious reasons, but 'twas not because I have not thought about it.

For me, years back I have thought very much upon the matter, but have never made up my mind irrevocably. Of course this solemn time has its due effect upon me, but I am always fearful of making resolutions under such circumstances which we will not be able to carry out hereafter. Added to the great bodily fatigue which we have had to undergo, the mental suspense is terrible, knowing as I do how much depends on the present struggle.

I have no doubt in my own mind but that this is the last great battle that will be fought if we prove victorious. The enemy fights with desperation. The battle of the day before yesterday (12th) was scarcely ever equalled in severity. The loss of the enemy is estimated at 40,000 men. I have never seen anything to equal it. Our men fought behind breastworks most of the time and so did not suffer as much as their opponents. Both sides were severely crippled however, and the day was followed by one of profound quiet yesterday, except as to shelling and sharpshooters, who are always active. . . .

Grant is the most obstinate fighter we have ever met. He has resolved to lose every man rather than retreat, which he knows is equivalent to our independence. He gives them whiskey before every fight and then sends them out to meet their death in a furious state of intoxication. Moreover, he gives them all, who are engaged in one of their reckless charges on our works, $50 bounty. Can you conceive people who will receive money to undertake such work in such a cause?

One evening last week, we were lying in reserve behind our front lines, when it gave way, letting the drunken villains in our works. We went forward with a yell, and drove them out at the point of the bayonet, when we came up to one of our batteries which the yankees had taken for the moment. Some of them were working the guns furiously, firing them upon their own retreating troops. When ordered to stop, they refused, saying they wanted to kill some of the rascals, which we let them do to their hearts' content as we did not understand the working of the guns, and they did. One of them blew a Lt. of my regiment to pieces with his gun after he (the yankee) had surrendered and was going to the rear.

May 16th, 1864: I wrote these pages some days ago hoping that I would have an opportunity of sending them off, none has occurred. We have not been engaged since I wrote, tho once we went out to make a flank movement in which we would have had some hard fighting. As it was raining hard, we were all glad when the scheme was abandoned.

Unfortunately we have had no mail since the fight began, which is a great trial, as the men are always more eager for letters at such times than at any other. Give my best love to all at home. I ask them all to write me.

Your aff. Bro.
EUGENE BLACKFORD

— ★ —

When he wrote this letter, Philip Powers* was serving as a captain in the Quartermaster Department, Cavalry Corps, Confederate Army of Northern Virginia. His letter home was written three days after his close friend General "J.E.B." Stuart was mortally wounded at the Battle of Yellow Tavern, Virginia.

Spotsylvania, Va.
May 15, 1864

MY DEAR WIFE:

The Sabbath morn opens upon us sadly this morning, and with a heart depressed with a deep and bitter grief I long to commune with some heart which can sympathize with me. We heard yesterday of the death of our noble leader, Genl. Stuart and the news has thrown a gloom upon us all. Since the death of the lamented Jackson, no event, no disaster, has so affected me. Jackson was a great loss to his country and to the cause. Genl. Stuart is a great

*Another letter by Philip Powers appears on page 11.

loss to his country. But to us, who have been intimately associated with him—and to me in particular—his loss is irreparable, for in him, I have lost my best friend in the army.

I cannot realize that he is *gone,* that I am to see his gallant figure, nor hear his cheering voice, no more. "God's will be done," a great man has fallen, and his faults are now swallowed up and forgotten in the recollection of his eminent virtues—his glorious valor and patriotism. May God in his mercy comfort his poor widow. My heart sorrows for her, as for one very near to me.

The two armies here still confront each other in line of battle, though there has been no serious engagement since Thursday, when Genl. Johnson's Division was repulsed and himself and many of his men captured. The position and some of the artillery was recovered but not the prisoners, though in the same day we repulsed every other attack.

It has been raining for three days, and you can hardly imagine how uncomfortable we are lying in the mud and wet every day. Fortunately, my neuralgia attack has worn itself out and affects me but very slightly, though I am worn out and wearied in mind with continued anxiety. Oh, if it could all end, and this terrible turmoil cease.

For nearly two weeks our men have been in line of battle, exposed to all the inclemency of the weather, fac[ing] the insufferable heat and now the drenching rains—and yet they stand and fight. The wounded and the maimed and the dying lie around on the cold wet ground. No dear ones near to minister to their wants —and the last breath is caught by the passing breeze and no listening ear of affection ever hears the sound. How long will a merciful God permit this war? And will the wail of the woe that rises from bloody battlefields never cease? . . .

Love to the children and kisses for the babes. God be with you, my good wife.

Ever Yours,
P. H. Powers

— ★ —

Frederick Pettit* served as corporal with Company C, 100th Pennsylvania Volunteer Infantry. His letter concerns the regiment's operations in Virginia at the Battle of the Wilderness and the Spotsylvania Courthouse Campaign.

Friday Evening
May 20th, 1864

DEAR PARENTS:

Supposing that you are anxious to hear from us, I thought I would write a few lines this evening. This is the first day of rest we have had since we crossed the Rapidan, which was on the 5th of May.

On the 6th, we were engaged in the battle of the Wilderness. We had but one man wounded in our company but lost several in the regiment. Our brigade was sent in the morning to Hancock's assistance on the left and we helped to repulse the rebels' last desperate charge on that part of the lines. The musketry was the most terrible I suppose ever heard. At least 30,000 muskets were being fired constantly for 1 hour and 40 minutes. We had three lines of breast works. Our loss was small. But little artillery was used.

On the night of the 7th, we marched to near Chancellorsville and remained in that vicinity until the morning of the 9th, when we marched toward Spotsylvania Court House and were the supporting division in driving the enemy to that place. Here we remained until the 12th, entrenching and skirmishing some all the time with the enemy. General Stevenson, who was commanding our division, was killed here on the 9th by a stray shot.

On the morning of the 12th, at daylight, our whole corps advanced against the enemy in front of Spotsylvania Court House. In a few hours, we had driven the enemy to their rifle pits. Our lines were now so extended that we had but a single line of battle

*Other letters by Frederick Pettit appear on pages 86 and 88.

in front of their works. To attempt to carry those works with a single line was simply impossible.

Our regiment lay in a thick pine woods about 300 yards from the enemy's rifle pits and losing heavily from their sharpshooters. About noon, our regiment was ordered to advance. We did so, driving the enemy's skirmishers before us. We soon came in sight of their rifle pits just over the crest of a ridge about 30 yards in front of us. We immediately opened fire upon them and they did the same. We could see nothing but the flash of their guns while they could see us plainly as we had no protection at all. Men were being killed and wounded faster than you could count them. Yet no one flinched until we were ordered back.

After falling back, we formed again where we were before charging. All day we continued to lose heavily from the fire of their sharpshooters. That night we built breast works and remained in the same position and moved about 3 miles to the left. Last night we were digging rifle pits until 11 o'clock and finished this morning at daylight. There was no enemy within gun shot of our front today and we rested. . . .

Company B, 170th New York Infantry, in the field during the Petersburg Campaign

Our regiment has lost about 200 men killed and wounded since we came to Virginia.

Your son,
FRED PETTIT

P.S. Let us not be uneasy about what may happen to us here, but put our trust in God. This fighting will last until the war is decided. As long as we live right, we can do our duty without fear. War is a sober thing and a soldier needs something more than mere courage to support him. Reading the Bible never seemed to afford me so much comfort as it does now. The only pleasant thing here is we have plenty to eat. There is fighting every day. Some of our recruits are not so brave here as they were at home.

Frederick Pettit was killed in action on July 9, 1864, at Petersburg.

— ★ —

John Gleichmann served as a private with Company A, 136th Indiana Volunteer Infantry.

———

Nolan Station, Hardin Co.
Kentucky
May 29, 1864

DEAR FAMILY AND ALL RELATIVES,

Sunday, it is a beautiful day but a lonesome day for me. We arrived here yesterday, it is 52 miles from Louisville, on the Louisville and Nashville railroad. Our regiment is divided up into small units between here and Louisville in order to guard the railroad from guerrillas. Our company is divided into 2 parts about 6 miles apart from each other. Our part has to protect the Nolan RR bridge. This bridge has been burned twice already by the guerrillas.

We are surrounded by rebels and guerrillas and have to be on guard. I think we have to stay here until our time is up. It is a beautiful area and has wonderful water to drink. The godlessness is great, cursing and whoring cries to heaven. Men from our company, yes even married ones, have gone to whore houses and paid 5 and 6 dollars per night. I was astonished. If their wives would know about it, it would cause terrific fights and maybe divorce. That's why I don't want to name them.

Oh, the temptation is great. The Christian is tested here. My daily prayer is, Lord, don't lead me into temptation but protect me from all sins. My firm decision is to be true to my savior to the end only by the grace of God. Thanks and praise to God, I am still healthy and well. This morning I left the turmoil and sought out privacy. There I read a chapter and became close to my God, and the Lord richly blessed me, but of love to my God and Savior I had to cry. I am not afraid because I know the Lord is with me.

I have to end my writing, I hope that these few lines will find you in good health as they left me. My lines are for all of you. I cannot write to everyone. . . .

Heartfelt greetings from me to all of you. I remain your true and loving, etc., till death,

J. M. GLEICHMANN

— ★ —

Aden Cavins* served as a lieutenant colonel with the 97th Indiana Volunteer Infantry. He wrote this letter to his wife four days after the Battle of Atlanta.

In the Field near Atlanta, Georgia
July 26, 1864

MY DEAR MATILDA:

I have just made a tour of the regiment and succeeded in getting material for writing you. . . .

It is not believed that this campaign will end until winter, unless the rebels are or shall be overwhelmed. We have no such hopes

*Other letters by Aden Cavins appear on pages 42 and 184.

in the army, unless, indeed, the enemy continue to assault us like they did on the 22nd. We give them credit for better sense, so we will have to do the attacking.

The fight on the 22nd was the most terrific and sanguinary affair ever witnessed in either army. Our brigade had a splendid position and fought for over four hours with the greatest coolness and courage, for our small brigade and a small brigade of the 17th Corps held in check at least 10,000 men from half past one until four o'clock, when re-inforcements were at hand.

The 97th fought in three different places and on each side of our works, for the attack was on front and rear. The rebel lines only lacked two hundred yards of closing around us in the hottest of the conflict. When our brigade was fiercely engaged—two regiments fronting south and one west, and two regiments northwest, with the enemy all around us except on the northeast—a caisson of horse attacked. The fight was so fierce that I did not notice the explosion. So a caisson wagon of the enemy exploded about one hundred and fifty yards on our front (it might have been two hundred yards) and none of us could tell the difference except by the smoke.

We killed a great many. At 5 o'clock, the 97th and 103rd Illinois were ordered to support the 3rd brigade, who were resisting the attack on our front while we were resisting the attack from our rear. We went on the double-quick for over a quarter of a mile, and found that the 3rd brigade had left that part of the line and the 48th Illinois were just leaving. They formed on our right, and we went into the works on the run, but the 48th soon gave way, and exposed our flank; the rebels swarmed across the works on our right and bore down on us. We killed, in front of our regiment, one colonel and major and one captain within fifteen feet of our lines. They were ordering our men out at the time. . . .

It is hard to say who did the most execution. The rebel colonel was shot full of holes twenty feet from where I was, the major and captain a little to the right and about the same time. Col. Treat-house was killed, which accounts for the 48th Illinois giving way and leaving my flank unprotected. They—the rebels—swarmed in so thick and fast that they captured five of Co. A. Two of Co.

A jumped on the rebel side of the works and made good their retreat. It was really safer on our front, for we had kept them at bay, than on our rear on the right of the regiment, for the rebels had crossed our works and were coming on us on each side of the works. . . .

Our losses were trivial, for during the first three hours and a half, we fired from a backbone of a ridge running through a field: part of the brigade fought while others carried rails, and in half an hour we had a splendid brigade. Every portion of the Army of the Tennessee that was engaged had been, during the day, driven out, except one small brigade of the 17th and our brigade—both together not larger than two regiments.

The running of wagons and stragglers, and the hauling off of batteries, made everything look blue, but not for one moment did

A dead Confederate soldier

I despair. At half past five o'clock we had regained all the ground lost on our right, and a strong line extended for one mile on our left, but swung back so as to leave our brigade on the angle. We had not given an inch.

I doubt whether the enemy has ever been punished to the same extent by so small a force. We had only one division of the 16th Corps, two divisions of the 17th Corps and our division (15th) and one brigade of Smith's until late in the evening, when the balance of Smith's and Osterhaus' had come into position. Part of them had been to Decatur.

The dead cover the country for one mile around. We had three killed, five wounded and five taken prisoners. It was the intention yesterday to send us off fifteen miles to fight another battle, but we are now occupying the rebel works that we took possession of on the morning of the 22nd, reversed so as to front Atlanta. We are resting, the rebels occasionally sending a shell in unpleasant proximity to our regiment, and their sharpshooters sending a musket ball in our midst. None have as yet been hurt by these, though nearly one hundred fall near us on each day.

I have taken cold, caught on the night of the 22nd by sleeping on the battlefield without any bed clothing. The fight lasted until after night.

My love to all.

— ★ —

Andrew McCornack served as a private with the 127th Illinois Volunteer Infantry. This letter was written during the Atlanta Campaign.

———

Near Atlanta
Aug. 1st, 1864

As I have nothing else to do, thought I would write a few lines to let you know that I am well. We have had another hard battle, the hardest fight I ever saw.

On the morning of the 26th, we left our works on the left and marched around to the left. The next day, we swung around to the right and formed a line of battle on a range of hills about three quarters of a mile from the enemy's works. We lay there about two hours. Then our regiment was ordered on the extreme right to protect our flank. It was Co. I's turn for skirmish.

We deployed as skirmishers and were watching for the johnnies when we heard the firing on the left. The rebs were coming with a heavy force. The fight began about noon. We kept a good watch, and pretty soon we saw them come and gave them the best we had in the wheelhouse, but still they came. We were obliged to fall back to our line of battle.

They still kept coming, until they got up within a few feet of us and were obliged to fall back. They were getting at our rear. They surrounded one of our posts and took three of the boys prisoners. They came very near taking our whole company, but when I saw that we were surrounded, I thought I would try and get away. I started as fast as Jim Shank's horses could travel. The rebs kept hollering, "Halt, you son-of-a-bitch," but I could not see it, and got away all right, and joined the regiment, which was pouring volleys into them the best they knew how.

Two regiments were brought to our support and formed on our right, and we were ordered to drive them back, and gain the ground we had lost. The boys started with a yell, pouring it among them as we went. They were obliged to fall back. The battle lasted until four o'clock, when they fell back to their works in disorder and gave it up as a bad job.

The next morning we found 640 dead in front of the 15th Corps. We could hear them carrying off wounded all night. Our corps lost not over 350 men, while that of the enemy was nearly three times as much. It was a fair, open, field fight, no breastworks of any kind, but we had good works before the next morning.

Yesterday we moved still further to the right and tried to draw the rebs out again but they thought it did not pay. We are about two miles from the R.R. running southwest from Atlanta. It won't be many days until it is in our hands. . . .

the chance to see *Harpers Weekly* of August 6th, you will see a very good picture of part of our battery commanded by Lt. Jackson. The mortar on the right of the picture is the one that I have had charge of most of the time.

I have written as much trash as you will care to cipher out at once so I will close with love.

Yours,
CHARLIE

— ★ —

John Sturtevant served as a lieutenant with the 2nd Division, 14th New Hampshire Volunteer Infantry.

———

Camp, 14th N.H.I., 2nd Div., A.C.
Halltown, Va.
August 9th, 1864

DEAR FRIENDS AT HOME,

It's so cool and comfortable this morning that I am sitting outside my tent on my valise and writing on a "hard tack" box, which by the way is a very convenient article. It serves for a table at meal times, a writing desk during the day, and at night I put it into the tent for a cupboard to put my plates and dishes in. I have often told you how much I enjoyed life in the field but never so much as now. It's a pleasant season of the year. We are in a delightful country and what is better than all, I am feeling well and strong.

My colored man I don't think I could get along without. He is a capital good boy, belongs to the Methodist church and is trusty and faithful. Every morning a little after light he comes and gives me a gentle shake and says "Lieutenant? Will you have tea or coffee this morning?" I tell him which I will have and turn over and go to sleep again. In about an hour he wakes me again and says, "Breakfast is most ready." I get up and wash and comb my hair and by that time he has the table all set. This morning I had baked beans, green apple sauce and hot biscuits with a quart of good tea.

I board with the company, paying them $5.00 per month. I draw the bulk of what I eat from them and then buy a few extras from the Commissary, such as sugar, tea, flour, ham, etc. I put the sugar in my sauce, make biscuit of the flour. You would hardly think one could bake biscuit in a tin plate, but my boy does. He puts them on a plate and sets it on the coals and then puts the other plate over them and puts coals on top of them: they bake in this way very quickly and nicely.

I did not not like the name of "Jim" for my boy, so I changed his name to "Eldridge" in honor of the grocery store man. He likes the change very well. I had a long talk with him last night on religious topics and found him to be quite well posted. He said he was glad I could talk with him and did not swear, drink or use tobacco. In the Regt. he used to be in—34th Ohio—"They swear powerful," he says, all but the Col., who was a good man.

Of matters military, there has been but little change since I last

A scene in the camp of the 3rd New Hampshire Infantry, Hilton Head, South Carolina

wrote you. Gen. Grant was here on the 7th and placed Gen. Sheridan in command. Yesterday 5000 of cavalry from the Army of the Potomac came, so we now have 10,000 cavalry and about 25,000 infantry.

The prevailing opinion is that we are to remain here and await Lee's movements; we are in a favorable position to move in any direction that may be required and are in condition to move rapidly and have a force large enough to do some executions. We are going to try and send a messenger to the right wing and get our mail, which will probably be up by the 11th.

When you write again, tell me if you have received all my letters. I think I have written seven or eight since I left N.H. I suppose you read the *Sentinel* regularly and that I shall get it when our mail comes. . . . I shall write often and hope to hear from you soon. Love to all. Ever your affectionate son,

JOHN

— ★ —

At the time of writing, Henry Morrison* was serving as a lieutenant with the 26th Virginia Infantry Battalion. His letter home was written the day after the Confederate defeat at the Third Battle of (Opequon Creek) Winchester, Virginia.

Fisher's Hill near Strasburg
Tuesday Evening
Sept. 20th, 1864

MY DEAR BROTHER:

We have had another great battle and by God's blessing and favor I am unhurt. My escape seemed almost miraculous. The yankees were all around me and almost ran over me, but this is of minor importance.

At daybreak, an unexpected attack was made upon Ramseur,

*Another letter by Henry Morrison appears on page 189.

who held the right of our line. Sheridan was present in person and directed the movements of the yankees. Ramseur was sorely pressed by immense columns of infantry whilst Breckenridge was occupying a line of skirmishers four miles in length upon the left of the line.

By eight o'clock, the fighting on Ramseur's line was desperate. Whole battalions of artillery were engaged on either side. Meantime Rodes and Gordon were hurrying at "double quick" from Stevenson's Depot on the Martinsburg Road to the assistance of the fighting columns. Ramseur held his position splendidly against repeated attacks and inflicted heavy loss upon the enemy. Rodes arrived upon the field and quickly put his men in position, but in a very short time this gallant officer was killed whilst superintending the disposition of his troops under a heavy fire.

The whole line pressed forward and swept the enemy like grasshoppers before them. Gordon, by this time, arrived and threw his men into the line, participating in the fighting. The firing increased in great measure, and orders were sent to Gen. Wharton to bring his division towards Winchester as rapidly as possible. The yankee cavalry in large force were on our left and we found it necessary to drive them off the road leading to Winchester. Fitz Lee came up and promised to attend to their cavalry and we pressed on towards the battlefield. At two o'clock, we were in position, having formed a junction with Gordon on the left. The enemy massed his columns and moved upon us. Firing over a stone wall, we literally piled the yankees in our front. For nearly an hour, we kept up a vigorous fire and repulsed every effort to storm our position.

I never saw our men act more splendidly. In the midst of the terrific fire, Col. Edgar exclaimed to me, "Is not it glorious to see them piled up that way?"—Gordon's men for some reason gave way on our right and fled in confusion far to the rear, leaving us to be enfiladed on flank and rear. Just at this critical moment, the cavalry of Fitz Lee was routed and the yankee cavalry came thundering down upon our left and rear. Having whipped the enemy in our front, we found ourselves cut off by the converging columns of infantry and cavalry, and order after order came to Col. Patton (commanding our brigade) to bring up his command if possible.

Facing about, we rushed back toward our main column, driving the yankees that had been rash enough to get between us and the rest of our line, killing many and capturing a number. The yankee cavalry were all mixed up with us and in many instances were knocked off their horses by the butt end of muskets in the hands of our men. Having no gun, I gathered a club and resolved to try to bring to the ground the first scoundrel who dared to halt me. It was the most exciting scene I ever beheld. I saw yankee cavalrymen shot by men whom they had halted and were trying to capture.

After a long and bloody retreat, we reached our line again, and joined Gordon once more, who had by this time rallied his men into a thin sort of line. The confusion was too great to be remedied and a stampede seemed inevitable. The men could not be rallied and a general retreat commenced, in which we lost heavily. Out of 16 officers, this battalion has only 4 left. 115 men are missing out of 245. Every field officer in our division was killed or captured save one. Col. Edgar is missing, and is supposed to be captured. Col. Patton was badly wounded. Genl's. Rodes and Godwin were killed, and Genl's. Fitz Lee and York were wounded. Our loss in killed, wounded and captured will reach 2500 or 3000, it is believed.

Last night we moved to Newtown and continued to this point this morning. The enemy are too badly pushed to press us. Their cavalry are feeling cautiously our front, but no infantry has yet appeared. Our men are in fine spirits and are anxious to be attacked here. Early was not prepared for an attack, and his defeat is felt to be altogether unnecessary. The men are eager to wipe out the shame which they think attaches to a defeat under any circumstances. . . .

I am very tired and sleepy. Yesterday's exertion and excitement were such as to weary both mind and body. We have no idea what our next movement will be. Tomorrow night may find us again at Winchester or it may find us nearer to Staunton.

> Affectionately your brother,
> H.P.M.

— ★ —

Lieutenant G. W. Davis served as a division quartermaster with the 11th Connecticut Volunteer Infantry. He wrote the letter printed below to the mother of Colonel Griffin Stedman.

————

> Point of Rocks, Virginia
> October 1st, 1864

Dear Madam,

Your letter of the 15th was received nearly ten days since, but owing to the excitement and hurry attendant upon the continual active operations and battles now being fought, I have found it impossible to spare time from my labors as Division Quartermaster to answer your letter. I feel truly grateful for—but entirely unworthy of—the thanks you bestow and if possible as proud to receive your thanks as I once was to enjoy the good opinion of your noble son.

I hesitated to break the seal of your letter, dreading to read the expressions of sorrow stricken woe which I was so sure to find. I very well knew that one of the first expressions which would meet my eye would be of regret and disappointment at not being able to know more of the circumstances attending the death of your son. I regret to say I fear I can give you few additional details of interest concerning that sad calamity. I will however, at the risk of causing you a renewal of pain by repeating what you have already heard, tell you what I know of the circumstances and incidents as they occurred.

About 3 o'clock or possibly later of the afternoon of the day on which he was shot, the firing of the pickets seemed to increase and soon became quite rapid, and the opinion among the general officers was that the enemy designed making an attack in force, or an attempt to penetrate our lines by assaulting them.

As a precautionary measure, the troops which had been lying about half a mile in the rear in reserve were ordered up and Col. Stedman's Brigade occupied a line within supporting distance of the pickets where the attack would be likely to take place. The troops after arriving here then lay down and sheltered themselves as well as possible from the enemy's fire.

Col. S. with his Asst. Adjt. General quietly and calmly walked up to the advanced line of trenches and endeavored to ascertain the cause of the firing. While [he was] thus walking and standing, Lt. Roberts once cautioned the Colonel against exposing himself to the enemy's fire, but he paid no attention to it or the bullets. While thus standing, a soldier was struck, seemingly on his side, whereupon the Colonel placed his hand on the corresponding spot upon his own person and said "If I am hit, I hope it may not be here."

Soon the firing slackened and then ceased entirely except an occasional discharge of shots between the pickets. The Col. turned to Lt. Roberts and said, "I don't believe we shall get a fight out of this disturbance." Soon Capt. Lawrence of Gen. Ames's staff came along and said, "Col., the General says that you will take your Brigade back to the ravine, let them cook their supper and get ready to go into the trenches tonight," and remarked that there was "going to be no fight today." The Col. inquired for Gen. Ames, saying that he wished to see him, whereupon Lawrence replied that the Gen. had gone out towards the left of the line, but he thought if they waited where they then were, Gen. Ames would soon pass.

The Col. now turned to Roberts and said, "Take the Brigade back to Camp, let them get supper and I will soon be along." After waiting a few minutes, Gen. Ames came up and commenced conversation with the Colonel. They were both standing in the trench and facing each other but a few feet apart, each resting an arm upon a sort of piling of boards which had been placed there by soldiers and were intended to be used as supports to which to fasten their shelter tents.

While [they were] thus standing—the Gen. with his right arm and the Col. with his left resting upon these boards—a bullet was heard to strike something and stop. All standing around heard it and Gen. Ames asked, "Who is hit?" The Col. immediately dropped his arm, and with his right hand unbuttoned his coat, took hold of his vest over the wound as if to remove the cloth from contact with the skin. It seems that some portion of his handkerchief had been struck and carried into the wound, and this the Col. drew out discolored with blood. He then turned and walked away, saying, "I believe I am hit."

He had not walked far before he began to feel weak. Gen. Ames on one side and Capt. Lawrence on the other supported him. He very soon lost his strength and gradually settled down, wishing to lie down. This he did, and turned to Gen. Ames and said, "Gen. Ames, I don't believe I shall recover from this."

A stretcher was now brought and he was taken a little distance to the rear, where the Surgeon of the 2nd Penn. Heavy Artillery examined the wound and made such a dressing as seemed to be needed. Dr. Whitcomb was sent for and soon arrived. What was then said and done Dr. W. has told you. Word was sent me also and in fifteen minutes I had ridden three miles and was at the Brigade Head Quarters.

The Col. was lying on a stretcher in his tent, and one glance at the Doctor's face convinced me that he expected the worst. When I arrived at Head Quarters, it was about 8 o'clock P.M. and the Col. seemed to be asleep but soon awoke and called for the Doctor and expressed himself as being in much pain. The Doctor gave him a little morphine, and the Col. asked, "How long is it likely that I shall live?" I did not hear the Doctor's reply, but have no doubt he told him the truth. He asked if it was likely he should suffer much, to which the Doctor replied—I think the Col.'s motive in asking this question was to learn if it was likely he would live long enough for his friends to be telegraphed for and arrive in time before he died. It seemed to me so at the time and I still think that was the thought which occupied his mind, for when the Doctor made reply, he seemed to heave a sigh and close his eyes —which at the moment I translated into a sigh of regret.

About this time I stepped into the tent, knowing that if I ever was to be again recognized by him, it must be immediately—he opened his eyes and said as calmly and coolly as usual, *"Well, Davis."* My only reply was, *"My Colonel."*

With his handkerchief, he wiped away a gathering tear and said, "I was too confident, Davis, too confident. I did not think that I should be struck, I have escaped so many times and when the danger was so much greater—it seems too bad to be shot in this insignificant skirmish." This was said in broken sentences, and he also remarked, "It gives me great pain to talk." I said, "The bullet first passed through a plank and might have lacked penetration and there may still be a chance of recovery," to which he replied, "So my career is ended," and then to the Doctor, "Oh! Put me to sleep now."

The Doctor gave him morphine which did not have the desired effect. With a countenance indicating great suffering, he again said, "Oh! Doctor, put me to sleep, put me to sleep quickly." The Doctor then saturated with chloroform a piece of lint and cotton and applied the same to his face—this did not have the desired effect and he was still restless, and indicated by his manner that he was suffering much pain. He asked to have his pillow arranged and raised himself for the purpose. I arranged his pillow and again he requested to be put to sleep.

More chloroform was administered, the effects of which soon became evident—one of his hands wandered wildly and grasped the bloody bandage on his breast as if to tear it away. A few broken utterances I heard, but could only understand one of them spoken in his usual tone and sounding quite familiar. They were spoken as if giving an order to a Staff Officer—the words were, "Let there be no delay." What they signified we can never know—whether they were intended for the Doctor relative to his being put to sleep, or whether his mind was wandering back to the exciting scenes of mortal conflict with the Brigade in the din of battle and making ready for a charge, or whether dreaming of his own dear friends at home, referring to their flying to his bedside to cheer his dying hours.

We can never know, but I have a fancy he was dreaming of his own loved friends. This was his last expression during the night as the chloroform had the desired effect, and he lay before us asleep with his bare breast encircled with the bloody bandage and one little spot more crimson than the rest marking the place where entered the fatal bullet, heaving and fading slowly, quietly and barely perceptibly. Then the Doctor looked at me and I looked at him and that was all—it was unnecessary that questions should be asked or information given. We both understood the situation.

I asked, "Who has telegraphed to his mother?" He replied, "I think that Mr. De Forest has." I found Mr. De Forest and learned that no telegram had been sent you. I asked the Doctor if it were likely he would live till morning. He replied, "I think quite likely, unless something unfavorable occurs soon." I immediately started for City Point and sent the despatch announcing the Colonel was very seriously wounded.

I arrived back at Petersburg next morning and lay down for an hour's rest, but was awakened from sleep in a few moments by a messenger sent by Dr. W. to inform me that Col. Stedman was dead and that he (Dr. W.) was then on the road with the body to be embalmed. You know the rest.

This is all I know and I think all that any one knows of the last hours of your son. I watched him with the most eager interest, knowing that I should be called upon to inform his family of appearance, words and looks.

G. W. DAVIS
LIEUT. & Q.M.

— ★ —

Edwin Hobson was serving as a lieutenant colonel with the 5th Alabama Volunteer Infantry when he wrote this letter to his fiancée after the Battle of Cedar Creek, Virginia, on October 19,

1864. In November he was promoted to the rank of colonel, for gallantry at Cedar Creek.

Headquarters, Battle's Brigade
New Market, Virginia
October 23, 1864

MY DEAR FANNY:

The day before yesterday, I wrote you a hurried letter with a pencil, which I fear you may not be able to read. However, you will see from it that I passed through the battle of the 19th safely. I could not permit a single day to end without writing to you to relieve any fears or anxiety you might have as to my being wounded. . . .

Before this, you have received accounts in the newspapers of our repulse at Strasburg on the 19th. Let me tell you something regarding General Ramseur's Division. This brigade particularly —Ramseur's Division was one of the three divisions that on the night of the 18th passed on the sides of the mountains, to take to the rear of Sheridan's army, and attacked the enemy at daylight.

Battle's Brigade became engaged after dawn. While driving to the enemy before them, General Battle was wounded about sunrise. General Ramseur rode up to me and told me to take command of the brigade and hold it on the turnpike until further orders. While [we were] resting there, the enemy shelled us heavily, killing and wounding several of my men. I soon got permission to attack the battery.

Upon giving my orders to the brigade to storm and take the battery, men bounded forward with a yell. In a few moments, they were in the midst of artillery, calling upon the yankees to surrender and, when [they failed] to do so, cutting them down with their swords or shooting them down. There we captured five pieces of artillery and our stand of colors. The artillery we captured belonged to six main artillery. I captured it with Battle's Brigade.

Just in the rear of this artillery, the enemy were found in a square and in the center of the square was a white flag. This I recognized as the headquarters flag of some general and immediately attacked it. The square was formed of at least three times as many men as I had, but my brave men attacked it so vigorously that we drove it back and scattered it in every direction until we encaptured many who were in the square.

The prisoners told us that General Sheridan himself was in the square and that the white flag was his headquarters flag. Had the troops on my right and left advanced as fast as I did, in all probability we would have captured his flag. But they did not, and after we had driven the square back some distance, broken and routed it, I had to move back the brigade and assist in driving back the troops that were immediately on my right and who had stubbornly and firmly resisted General Wharton.

I directed my movements on them, the enemy's right flank, and in less than ten minutes we routed them as completely as troops ever were. We advanced some four or five hundred yards and then halted to reform the line. While [we were] halted, General Ramseur dashed up to me and in a loud voice said, "Colonel Hobson, old fellow, you are still in the front," and then pulling off his hat said, "Hurray for you" . . .

Late in the evening, when the enemy made a general advance along our entire front, they advanced in my front with both infantry and cavalry at the same time, shelling us furiously. The brave and undaunted men I commanded, true to themselves and knowing they could drive back any force brought against them, received this attack and hurled it back as they had done throughout the entire day. The troops on our left, however, were not so fortunate and soon we saw General Gordon Kershaw's men fleeing to the rear as precipitously as had the enemy in front of us, just a moment before—soon the enemy had a flank fire on us, but still we remained at our post. I did not see a man in my brigade give way until General Ramseur rode up to me and told me to move the brigade back.

I then moved to the brow of the hill immediately in my rear and there remained until he (General R.) came to me and again told me to move still farther back. We then retired to the next hill and repulsed every attack the enemy made on us. While here, General Ramseur was wounded. I was near him fifty or a hundred yards in front of him. The men on our left continued to give way. Soon thousands of men passed through my ranks. Here the army became routed and no stand was made after that.

Had they not poured through my ranks and thus disorganized the brigade, I believe firmly I could have driven back the entire force that was then coming against us and before which our entire army was so ingloriously fleeing. I made every exertion to stop all men I saw, but it did no good. They did not heed me, but passed on to the rear. The few men of my brigade I saw I stopped, but no others.

Humiliated beyond expression, we retired to Fishers Hill to tell all of our disgrace. So far as I am concerned personally, I have nothing to regret. Several officers have told me that had General Ramseur not been wounded, or had he escaped being captured soon after he was wounded, that they had no doubt that he would have done everything to have had me promoted, at once, to the rank of brigadier general. In losing General R., I have lost a good friend. I trust he may live and be returned to us. No general ever handled a division with better skill and no soldier ever behaved more bravely than he did on that day. . . .

I will write again in a few days. In the meantime hope to receive a letter from my own Fanny.

Truly yours,
E. L. HOBSON

— ★ —

Cyrus Lewis served with the 1st Missouri Engineers.

———

Head Qrts. 1st Regt. Engrs.
Mo. Vols.
Atlanta, Ga.
Nov. 3, 1864

DEAR FATHER AND MOTHER,

After a strong time of anxious waiting, I have again received from your hand a welcome letter bringing the pleasing intelligence of your good health and well being. Ah! If there is anything that will afford consolation and comfort to worn and wearied soldiers, it's the reading of communications from parents and loved ones at home. It inspires the soldiers with more confidence and energy to press onward toward the grand ultimatum of this *awful* but *magnificent* warfare.

Awful, I say, because of the great destruction of life, and the deep mourning of the land. *Magnificent* because it is accomplishing the abolition of (that foul stain) human slavery and planting and cultivating in its stead the principals of true radical reform. Hence the *great* and *paramount* object the people should have in view is supporting the present administration and carrying to the presidential chair the very man who had presided over the government during the last four years of trial and warfare and who has always been found at the helm guiding and directing the great ship of our country.

The present issue is one of the greatest and most important in the history of our country or that the land has ever known. Here is life or death to our republican form of government and free institutions. If McClellan is elected, we will have peace but it will be upon the recognition of the damnable rotten Confederacy of the south. If such should be the case, I and a thousand would spend the rest of our days in fighting against it.

We have lived, prospered and been protected under a free government, and we wish to preserve the same for the welfare and happiness of our posterity. The welfare of millions yet unborn is dependent upon us, and thus far we are responsible for their welfare. It behooves us then to do all in our power to sustain the government. It is to be one on the 8th day of this month.

Father, I want no greater consolation than to know that you are going to support the government. If I have the privilege of voting, I am going to cast my vote for Lincoln and Johnson and for the people. I have read and studied the Chicago Platform, and I pronounce it treason of the darkest hue. They call it democracy and are holding it up to the people as democracy and are trying to make the people think it's right by crying *peace, peace,* and talking about free speech, but when Mr. Murphy of Maryland opposed the nomination of McClellan at Chicago, they hissed him down and cried put him out, put him out. But since he could not say all that he wished to until he had knocked down two or three of his fellow democrats, I think it is a fair demonstration of their democracy.

It is like a thief feigning to be a clergyman or a wolf in lamb's clothing. It seems that they have taken upon themselves the responsibility of damning to all eternity the black abolitionists and have gone so far as to pronounce the federal soldiers hessians and hirelings right in their face and, yes, of the militia at Chicago, and there was no resistance made. If it has come to such a test that militia will give consent to such views and proceedings by remaining silent, then it is high time that we were waking up to a quicker and keener sense of the duties involving upon as American citizens and soldiers for the maintenance of government and its laws, but perhaps I have already written too much upon this subject. Though it is one that I am deeply interested in, I will drop it, feeling that the hand of kind providence is lifted in behalf of our country.

We are now fitted out for a campaign of fifty days but we have no knowledge of our destination. We will no doubt be entirely cut off from communicating with our friends for a time. Therefore you must not think it strange if you don't hear from me for some time. . . .

Yours In Truth,
CYRUS H. LEWIS TO
SAMUEL C. AND MARTHA LEWIS
AND ALL TRUE UNION PEOPLE

— ★ —

Andrew Moon served as a private with Company C, 104th Ohio Volunteer Infantry. This letter was written four days after the Confederate defeat at the Battle of Franklin, Tennessee, where

*some of the bloodiest and most tragic fighting of the war oc-
curred.*

Nashville, Tenn.
Sabbath, Dec. 4, 1864

SISTER SADE,

Some time has passed since I wrote you a letter and part of it
a bloody time with me, but I am very thankful that I have been
as lucky as not to receive a scratch.

To begin, I must relate from the end of the 29th Nov. That eve,
after a brisk skirmish with the rebs, our forces commenced to
withdraw from Columbia, Tenn. We marched all night, and in the
morning about daylight we found ourselves at Franklin, Tenn., a
distance of 23 miles—a pretty good night's march. We got breakfast at Franklin, then went to fortifying the place. We marched all

Union soldiers in the trenches before Petersburg, December 1864

day until about 4 o'clock P.M., when the Johnnies thought they would try us.

On they came in three lines, driving our skirmishers and front line in ahead of them. We let them get up within about 400 yards of our marks. Then we opened fire on them with cannon and muskets, slaying hundreds. I tell you, it was but a few of them that reached the works and what did surrendered and came in. There was a few of them got up in safety and climbed over the marks and commenced a hand to hand fight with our men behind the works, but our men would just turn their muskets and beat their brains out right on the spot.

There was a steady firing kept up until after dark. After it ceased a little, I went over in front of the works to see what we had done. Well, for 400 yards in front, I could hardly step without stepping on dead and wounded men. The ground was in a perfect slop and mud with blood and, oh, such cries that would come up from the wounded was awful. Oh, how they suffered that night was terrible, they had to lay just as they were shot down all night without anything done for them. I think they will long remember the last night of November 1864. Co. C had 4 men killed and 5 men wounded. . . .

After the battle that night, we fell back from Franklin and left the dead for them to bury—that is, their own dead. We lost about 700 men in killed, wounded and missing. They lost about 6,000 killed and wounded and about 1,500 prisoners. Our corps and the 4th was all that was engaged.

We are now stationed at Nashville. There is some cannonading today from the fort. Their line of marks is about two miles in front but we have some guns that can easily throw shells to them. They threw a 64-pound ball. I tell you, they make a loud refrain when they go off. I don't know if they will attack us here or not. If they do, they will get worse whipped than they did at Franklin. . . .

Excuse this hastily written letter and all mistakes from your affectionate Brother,

A.J.

— ★ —

Eugene McWayne served as a private with the 127th Illinois Volunteer Infantry.

————

Near Savannah, Ga.
Dec. 19th, 1864

DEAR MOTHER AND SISTERS:

. . . We arrived here safe and sound. We had a pleasant trip, leaving Atlanta the 15th of Nov., arriving here the 8th of Dec. We did not cross the river until the 11th. We had plenty of yams, molasses, fresh pork and mutton, corn meal, chickens, turkeys and geese. We lacked for nothing. It was a march of plenty.

The people along the road would tie their horses and mules in swamps, drive their cattle, sheep and hogs onto islands in the swamp. Buried all of their clothes, corn, salt pork, jewelry, money—well, in fact, everything they had in the house except themselves. But they were found by the D—— Yankees, after all.

You would ask how the Yankees knew where it was. Well, they would come across a pretty soft piece of ground. The first thing they would do would be to pull the ramrod out of their guns and run it down into the ground until it struck something that sounded like a board, or iron. Then they would commence digging for it. I dug up a valise on a plantation where we stopped overnight and found $16,300.00 in Confederate money. I will send a $5 bill home.

Well, I almost forgot one thing that will be amusing. The boys were hunting around a plantation to see what they could find. Well, they came across some fresh dirt, so they pushed their ramrods down. It struck a board, so they commenced digging. Well, to their surprise, someone beneath the board yells out, "Hold on, let me out, I will surrender." Well, they dug on till they could get hold of the board and pulled it out. And there was a *Johnny.* He had dug a hole in the ground, placed a board over it with a hole in it, so he could get air. Then he covered it over with dirt, but was careful to keep the hole open to get a supply of fresh air. This was done by the aid of the women folks, I suppose. You may bet he was a scared *Johnny*.

We are having oysters and fish a plenty. Oysters in the shell, of course, for we have to rake them out of their beds ourselves. We are camped on a plantation owned by Dr. Chevers. He had about 2,000 acres of rice in the shock when we came here, but we are gathering it as fast as two or three hundred six-mule teams can draw it. We have four teams drawing to feed our cattle. We have about 800 head now, so you can't say but what I have walked in the rice fields, or raked up the oyster beds, and have seen salt water. Just think of having an oyster supper at any time you please.

Sherman advances his lines today. I suppose I will spend the holidays in or near Savannah. . . .

I have seen a full blooded African on this march. We have a dance here on this plantation most every night. There is between forty and fifty little negroes. They pat, dance and sing at the same time. It is worth more to see them than all of your theaters or circuses or prayer meetings in the whole North.

> My respects to all,
> EUGENE

— ★ —

Luther Rice Mills served as a second lieutenant with the 26th Virginia Volunteer Infantry. His letter was written during the last leg of the Petersburg Campaign, which lasted from June 15, 1864 to April 3, 1865.

———

Trenches Near Crater
March 2nd, 1865

BROTHER JOHN:

Something is about to happen. I know not what. Nearly everyone who will express an opinion says Gen'l Lee is about to evacuate Petersburg. The authorities are having all the cotton and tobacco moved out of the place as rapidly as possible. This was commenced about the 22nd of February. Two thirds of the Artillery of our Division has been moved out. The Reserved Ordnance Train has been loaded up and is ready to move at any time. I think Gen'l Lee expects a hard fight on the right and has ordered all this simply as a precautionary measure. Since my visit to the right I have changed my opinion about the necessity for the evacuation of Petersburg. If it is evacuated Johnson's Division will be in a bad situation for getting out. Unless we are so fortunate as to give the Yankees the slip many of us will be captured. I would regret very much to have to give up the old place. The soiled and tattered Colors borne by our skeleton Regiments is sacred and dear to the hearts of every man. No one would exchange it for a new flag. So it is with us. I go down the lines, I see the marks of shot and shell, I see where fell my comrades, the Crater, the grave of fifteen hundred Yankees, when I go to the rear I see little mounds of dirt, some with headboards, some with none, some with shoes protruding, some with a small pile of bones on one side near the end showing where a hand was left uncovered, in fact everything near shows desperate fighting. And here I would rather "fight it out." If Petersburg and Richmond [are] evacuated—from what I have seen and heard in the army—our cause will be hopeless. It is useless to conceal the truth any longer. Many of our people at home have become so demoralized that they write to their husbands, sons and brothers that desertion *now* is not *dishonorable.* It would be impossible to keep the army from straggling to a ruinous extent if we evacuate.

I have just received an order from Wise to carry out on picket tonight a rifle and ten rounds of cartridges to shoot men when they desert. The men seem to think desertion no crime and hence never shoot a deserter when he goes over—they always shoot, but never hit. I am glad to say that we have not had but four desertions from our Regiment to the enemy. . . . Write soon.

> Yours truly,
> L. R. MILLS

— ★ —

J. Webster Stebbins served as a first sergeant with Company I, 9th Vermont Volunteer Infantry. His letter was written the day Federal troops entered and took control of Richmond, Virginia, the capital of the Confederacy. The 9th Vermont was one of the first units into the city.

Richmond, Virginia
April 3rd, 1865

DEAR MOTHER:

The fated city has fallen and the black clouds of smoke from its burning ruins are rising to the heavens, and the pickets from the 9th Vermont were the first ones into the rebel capital.

We are in the works in the suburbs of the city. The enemy evacuated last night, and I have heard of no fighting at all today this side of the river. The rebels fired the arsenal Co. and the bridge across the James River also. We heard the shell in the arsenal bursting for half an hour.

The country is a fine looking one; some fine residences. So far as I have seen, the citizens are glad to see the Union soldiers coming. . . .

At last dispatch from Grant, we learn that they had captured some 15,000 prisoners and any quantity of guns, etc. It was just five minutes of five this morning when we halted in this fort and planted our colors on the parapet, giving three cheers for the *fall of Richmond.*

Do not know when I will get this into the mail, but hope it is soon. My regards to all and much love for yourself. Write soon and direct to Richmond, Va.

Your Affectionate Son,
J. W. STEBBINS

— ★ —

John Lightner was a hospital steward who served as a private with the 200th Pennsylvania Volunteer Infantry. He wrote home on the day of Lee's surrender.

———

Nottoway C.H., Va.
Sunday, April 9th, 1865

MY DEAR MOTHER:

I really think the first thing I ought to do is to beg pardon for not writing you for so long. The first chance to send a letter since we started however was this morning, but I had none ready.

Have not the last weeks been glorious one[s]? You must be nearly wild with excitement. I know I am, and I don't know near as much as you do. I feel just like hurrahing every time I think of it. The end is surely near. Where the rebels are is now the question. I don't believe they are of much account anywhere.

Yesterday afternoon, I met a small squad of over 8,000 going to the rear under guard, and they reported that Lee only had about 20,000 with him in any sort of shape and that is almost nothing in front of our army. Our boys are jubilant I tell you, anxious and eager to push on. I may be over-sanguine but I am really looking for the close of this long and desperate struggle in the course of a month. I don't see how it can last.

But perhaps you are particularly interested in the personal movements of your absent boy. You can get all general details of movements through the newspapers.

Well, after my scribble in the old camp on Monday morning, I went again to [the] hospital. About noon, all were packed and we took our place in the passing column through our works across the long-contested middle ground, through the rebel lines, which are if anything more wonderful and intricate than our own, and on into Petersburg, the town whose steeples I have been looking at for almost ten months. No one could help thinking in passing through the reb lines, if they could not hold such fortifications as they had there, surely they cannot make a stand anywhere. The fighting is almost over.

It was hard to realize that we really were in Petersburg. I remained there all afternoon, riding up one street and down another, stopping occasionally at some house. It is really a very pleasant city and by far the largest that I have yet seen in Virginia. The inhabitants were rather shy. Most of them did not appear particularly well pleased, but our troops were feeling gay and we made the old town ring again with good old Union music. Our troops all filed out along the Southside R.R. Thus far we have been following it right along. I suppose in a day or two it will be in running order up to this point and probably beyond.

Our division had been engaged all the time in that meanest of all ways of marching wagon guard and bringing up the rear of our whole wagon train. I have occasionally heard the sounds of fighting away in our front, but never near enough to be at all engaged. 'Tis a very safe position and in fact a pretty responsible one, though there is but little honor, credit or glory in it. We have been taking it very leisurely, we are only about 45 miles from Petersburg now. We have had seven nights marching nearly all the time, though never more than five or ten miles at a time.

We have had most beautiful weather ever since we started and the country looks pretty. 'Tis a better country here than on the other side of the river, many large plantations, but very few what I call comfortable houses. I do think they are as a class the most miserable set of people that I ever saw. They do not seem to have the least idea of what decent living is. Of course there are a few exceptions but only about enough to prove the general rule.

The orchards are all in full bloom, flowers beginning to appear and the grain fields are beautifully green. So far we are having a beautiful country trip. Last night was the first that has really seemed to me like actual campaigning. The first night that I have slept in a tent. I have had a house every other night and all but one good bed to sleep in. . . .

Love to father, self and all folks as ever,

Your Affectionate Son,
JOHN

— ★ —

James Coburn* served as a corporal with the 141st Pennsylvania Volunteer Infantry.

<hr/>

On the road to Lynchburg, Virginia
April 10, 1865

DEAR ONES AT HOME:

Hip! Hip! Hurrah! General Lee surrendered yesterday. It was the greatest day that I ever saw.

We have had one of the hardest campaigns that I ever saw—night and day—but the results how glorious!

I am writing on rebel paper captured in General Pickett's headquarters train. The 141st has not had a man killed and but few wounded.

Federal soldiers at Appomattox Courthouse, April 1865

*Another letter by James Coburn appears on page 127.

The papers will tell you more than I can about what we have done and are doing. "There's a good time coming." My health is good and spirits never better. Love to all, more anon.

J.P.C.

— ★ —

William Hamblin served as a private with Company K, 4th Massachusetts Heavy Artillery.

Fort Barnard
April 16, 1865

MY DEAR WIFE,

I suppose you have all heard the dreadful news of the murder of the President ere this. It does not seem possible that he could have been killed in the manner he was, after having for the last four years passed through so much danger with his life in his hand, to be at last struck down by a drunken, miserable play actor, a dissipated fool who did not know when he had done the deed and cried "Revenge for the South" that he had killed a man who had that day been kindly urging the mild treatment of the rebels and who has on more occasions than one risked his reputation for honesty of purpose to shield the South from the just desserts that she was receiving and has always stood ready to listen to any decent proposals for terminating the war.

In killing the President the South has lost their *best* friend. With the feeling that has been awakened by the assassination of the President, the treatment that the Vice President who succeeds him received at the hands of the rebels in Tennessee, the feeling that must prevail in the Armies of Grant, Sherman and Sheridan and the Navy everywhere—I am inclined to think the South and all who sympathize with her will meet with rather harsh treatment hereafter. If the inhabitants of the South are not reduced to a worse situation than the Irish under the English Government, then I am mistaken in the signs of the times. I am afraid they don't realize what is in store for them, but they will soon be undeceived if Johnson has his own way and I hope to God he will!!

It seems so sad right in the midst of our rejoicings at the prospects of a speedy peace, and while Lee is doing what he can to put a stop to the slaughter of innocent men on his part, that this thing should have happened. There is but one response to this, the last argument of "Southern Chivalry," and that is a cry for vengeance, and you may be sure it will come. Thank God the President, in using his influence in the selection of his chief officers of State, has left the Government in such hands that we need not fear any loss of National dignity. The Government will go on in spite of this terrible bereavement. If the South will not learn what they have lost, they will be made to drink the dregs of the cup that Lincoln would have spared them, and it is my desire that they should. . . .

All the flags on all the forts today are at half mast, every citizen who is caught within our lines is picked up and trotted off to the Guard House, Martial Law is proclaimed in Washington, we are kept sleeping at night with our equipments on all ready to start for Washington or Richmond as the case may be at a moment's notice—as Theodore Parker used to quote, "The mills of God grind slow but they grind exceeding fine," and if the South isn't ground down after this, I am much mistaken. I suppose you read all the particulars in the papers at home but I will try and get you a paper here and send it. You have no idea of the bitter, revengeful feeling that prevails. . . .

Affectionately Yours,
W. A. HAMBLIN

INDEX

PERMISSIONS
ACKNOWLEDGMENTS

Letters written by James Binford, John Esten Cooke, Thomas Elder, Edwin Hobson, James Holloway, John W. Holloway, Florence McCarthy, and David A. Weisiger are from the Manuscript Collection of the Virginia Historical Society; letters written by David Ash, Samuel Beardsley, Luther Bradley, James Coburn, Henry Curtis, John Gleichmann, Robert Goodyear, Andrew McCornack, Eugene McWayne, Henry Morrison, Horatio Newhall, Frederick Pettit, and Chester Tuttle are from the Collection of the Department of the Army, U.S. Army Military History Institute; letters written by William Darst, Eugene Blackford, Philip Powers, Theodore Compass, Amos Steere, Benjamin Rober, Constantine Hege, Henry Pearson, Hayward Morton, Edward Wood, John Lewis, Frank Phelps, Charles Smith, John Sturtevant, G. W. Davis, Andrew Moon, J. Webster Stebbins, Cyrus Lewis, John Lightner, and William Hamblin are reprinted by kind permission of Mr. Lewis Leigh, Jr., Lewis Leigh Collection, Department of the Army, U.S. Army Military History Institute; letter written by Lt. John H. Burnham dated October 4, 1862, is from the Collection of Letters written by John Henry Burnham and Nathan Mayer, 1862–1865 (973.77, B933, Main Vault), in the State Archives, History and Genealogy Unit, Connecticut State Library; letter written by

PERMISSIONS ACKNOWLEDGMENTS

James Hamner is from the Collection of the West Tennessee Historical Society; letter written by Charles Bowditch is from the Collection of the Massachusetts Historical Society; letter written by William R.M. Slaughter is reprinted by kind permission of Thomas Nash; letter written by David Wyatt Aiken is from the David Wyatt Aiken Papers of the South Caroliniana Library, The University of South Carolina; letter written by Henry T. Owen dated July 18, 1863, is from the Personal Papers Collection (Accession 28143), Archives Branch, Virginia State Library and Archives, Richmond, Virginia; letter written by General Alpheus Williams published in From the Cannon's Mouth, *edited by Milo M. Quaife, Detroit: Wayne State University Press and the Detroit Historical Society, 1959; letters written by Aden Cavins published in* The War Letters of Aden G. Cavins; *letters written by Warren Freeman published in* Letters from Two Brothers to Their Family at Home in Cambridge, Massachusetts, *1871; letters written by Spencer Glasgow Welch published in* A Confederate Surgeon's Letters to His Wife, *1911; letters written by Edward Ketcham and John Ketcham published in* Fighting Quakers, *edited by A.J.H. Duganne, 1866; letter written by Oliver Wilcox Norton published in* Army Letters, 1861–1865, *1903; letters written by Frederick Bartleson published in* Letters from Libby Prison, *edited by Margaret W. Peelle, 1956; letters written by Samuel Nichols published in* Your Soldier Boy Samuel, *edited by Charles Sterling Underhill, 1929.*

Grateful acknowledgment is made to the following for permission to reprint previously published material: Rutgers University Press: *excerpts from* The Civil War Letters of General Robert McAllister, *edited by James I. Robertson, Jr. Copyright © 1965 by Rutgers, The State University. Reprinted by permission;* University Press of Mississippi: *excerpts from* My Dear Nellie, *edited by William Cash and Lucy Somerville Howorth. Reprinted by permission;* North Carolina Division of Archives and History: *letter written by Luther Rice Mills, dated March 2, 1865, published in the July 1927 issue of the* North Carolina Historical Review. *Reprinted by permission;* Georgia Historical Quarterly: *letter written by Thomas R. Lightfoot published in Volume 25 (1941) of the* Georgia Historical Quarterly. *Reprinted by permission.* University of Texas: *Letters reprinted from* This Infernal War: The Confederate Letters of Sgt. Edwin H. Fay, *edited by Bell Irvin Wiley. Copyright © 1958, by permission of the University of Texas Press.*

All photographs are from the picture libraries of the National Archives and the Department of the Army, U.S. Army Military History Institute.